Dr. D. James Kennedy
and
Coral Ridge Ministries Media, Inc.

present this special volume to you from

THE KENNEDY COLLECTION
1997

Truths That
Transform

Christian Doctrines
for Your Life Today

Expanded Edition

D. JAMES KENNEDY

Fleming H. Revell
A Division of Baker Book House
Grand Rapids, Michigan 49516

©1974, 1996 by D. James Kennedy

Published by Fleming H. Revell
a division of Baker Book House Company
P.O. Box 6287, Grand Rapids, MI 49516-6287

Fifth printing, April 2005

Printed in the United States of America

Library of Congress Cataloging-in-Publication Data

Kennedy, D. James (Dennis James), 1930–
    Truths that transform : Christian doctrines for your life today /
D. James Kennedy.—expanded ed.
        p.   cm.
    Includes bibliographical references and index.
    ISBN 0-8007-5609-6 (paper)
        1. Theology, Doctrinal—Popular works. I. Title.
BT77.K277   1996
230—dc20   96-19548

Unless otherwise marked, Scripture quotations are from the King James Version of the Bible.

Scripture quotations marked RSV are taken from the Revised Standard Version of the Bible, copyright 1946, 1952, 1971, and 1973 by the Division of Christian Education of the National Council of the Churches of Christ in the United States of America.

For current information about all releases from Baker Book House, visit our web site:
http://www.bakerbooks.com

To my daughter Jennifer
who has been a source of continual joy

Contents

Preface

In this age of "soda-fizz" theology, it seems to me that there is a great need for more substantial biblical and theological foundations—lest the bubbles burst. In a culture that has become almost entirely experientially oriented, there is a crucial need for the eternal verities of God's Word. I have, therefore, endeavored to set forth in these pages in popular fashion some of the great truths of the historic Christian faith.

These are *Truths That Transform!* The Coral Ridge Presbyterian Church of Fort Lauderdale, Florida, where it has been my joy and privilege for the past thirty-seven years to minister for Christ, has been for many the proving ground of these truths. They do indeed transform! This church has been noted for the evangelistic ministry of its laypeople. Many have asked, "How are such laypeople produced?" I am certain that good spiritual nutrition is a vital factor. The great old truths of the faith put iron in people's backbones and enable them to stand tall for Christ. Herein are contained some of the great teachings of Christianity that God has used throughout centuries to bless lives, transform people, and build His church.

Over the many months during which these chapters were prepared, a vast number of sources were consulted, including Augustine, Martin Luther, John Calvin, John Knox, Charles Hodge, A. A. Hodge, Robert Dabney, Charles Shedd, Robert Webb, John Murray, Lorraine Boettner, John Gerstner, Abraham Kuyper, Alexander Keith, Carl F. H. Henry,

Francis Schaeffer, and many others too numerous to be mentioned. I am greatly indebted to all of these people for the light they have shined upon God's Word. Ultimately, we have endeavored to be faithful to the Holy Scriptures, which are the only infallible rule of faith and practice and which are to be the final authority in all matters of religion.

I would like to express my deep appreciation to Cay Hunter, Virginia Shaw, and my excellent secretary, Ruth Rohm, for their fine work in editing the manuscript. Of course, whatever errors or mistakes there may be are fully my responsibility.

I send this manuscript off with the heartfelt prayer that God may be pleased to use it for the upbuilding and strengthening of His kingdom and the glory of His name.

Soli Deo Gloria!

D. James Kennedy, Ph.D.

1

The Sovereignty of God

Remember the former things of old: for I am God, and there is none else; I am God, and there is none like me, declaring the end from the beginning, and from ancient times the things that are not yet done, saying, My counsel shall stand, and I will do all my pleasure: Calling a ravenous bird from the east, the man that executeth my counsel from a far country: yea, I have spoken it, I will also bring it to pass; I have purposed it, I will also do it.

Isaiah 46:9–11

Your God is altogether too human," wrote Luther to the famous Renaissance humanist scholar Erasmus. I feel certain the great Dutch scholar was greatly offended at such an accusation, but history and a casual investigation of Scripture reveal the accusation to be true. In our day, J. B. Phillips has hurled the same accusation at humankind in the title of his book *Your God Is Too Small.* With this thought in mind, I want to ask the question, Who rules the world in which you live—the world you read about on the front page of your newspaper? How big is your God?

I realize that the sovereignty of God is not a popular subject. It never has been and never will be. Since the beginning of creation, the creature has sought to usurp the place of the Creator. This was seen in Lucifer, the angel of light, who tried to become like God and take upon himself the prerogatives of God. For this reason, he was cast out of heaven and a great multitude of angels with him. It was this same sin that brought the whole human race into its present disgraceful and depraved condition. Man wanted to usurp the authority of God and be the god of his own life. Man was unwilling to listen to the words of Him who said, "Thus far shalt thou go and no further. Thou shalt not eat" (see Gen. 2:17). But the creature reached out a rebellious hand, took, ate, and died!

The skeptic H. G. Wells said that the world is like a great stage production produced and managed by God. As the curtain goes up, all is lovely to behold. The characters are fantastically beautiful—a delight to both eye and ear. All goes well until the leading man steps on the hem of the leading lady's dress. She then trips over a chair and knocks over a lamp which pushes over a table into the side wall. This knocks over the back scenery, which brings the whole thing crashing down in chaos on the heads of the actors! Meanwhile, behind the scenes, God, the Producer, is frantically running to and fro, pulling strings and shouting orders, trying desperately to restore order to the chaos. But—ah!—alas! He's unable to do so! Poor God! This is the God of modern man, a very little, limited God. "Either God is not good or He is not powerful," said one unbeliever, "otherwise the world could not be in the mess it's in." Since most people are unwilling to believe God is not good, they conclude He is not all powerful. He's doing the best He can, but His best isn't good enough! He is the God who tries and fails. Which horn of this dilemma do you choose?

May I suggest an alternative? The reason for the mess the world is in is not that God is not good, or not able. The problem is that humankind is not good or able. Consider for a moment a trip to hell. After arriving and surveying the awful scene, you would see nothing but misery and woe. You might conclude that God is not good or able, otherwise He would not allow such a place of misery. But your conclusion would be wrong. It is precisely because God is good, holy, just, and because He is all powerful, that these wicked, sinful, and rebellious people have been cast into hell.

Many people worship a limited God, but close scrutiny reveals that He is not the God of Scripture. The God of the Bible is the omnipotent Creator and Ruler of the world!

If the Old Testament presents anything of God, it presents three attributes: First is the *omnipotence of God*. He has all power and therefore His plan will be worked out. Second is the *holiness of God*. He is holy and therefore His plan, which will be and is being worked out, is one which is morally right. Third is the *personality of God*. He is not some mere omnipotent force as the fatalist would maintain, but a Person, who is infinite and whose attributes are love, mercy, wisdom, righteousness, justice, goodness, and truth. God is a Person who is all powerful and all holy.

The biblical picture is not one of fatalism, because fatalism puts the world's fate into the hands of an impersonal force. The Bible puts the world's fate into the hands of God the Father, who is all righteous, all wise, and all merciful. Fatalism rules out all second causes, whereas the Bible establishes them. Philosophers have never been able to reconcile human freedom with divine sovereignty. The Bible declares man, in a certain sense, is free. He is free to do whatever he *pleases*, though he is not free in his natural state to do what he *ought* because he is bound by sin and thus is the bondslave of sin. But he is free to do whatever he wants. This is man's great problem: His heart and mind are depraved.

Many people see the world as a driverless chariot, horses running wild, reins flapping in the wind, about to plummet off the edge of the road into the abyss. The Scripture presents a God who has the reins of this world firmly in His hands, who is in absolute control of all things, and who is working out His perfect plan for the world. The Scripture says: "My counsel shall stand, and I will do all my pleasure . . . yea, I have spoken it, I will also bring it to pass; I have purposed it, I will also do it" (Isa. 46:9–11). Sinful people flaunt the so-called autocracy of their own human will. They suppose themselves to have veto power over the plans of the Almighty.

Some believe that God submits and man permits, that God can do only that which man allows Him. How ludicrous to think that Almighty God, who by His very word caused the galaxies of the universe to leap into being, should be governed by His creation—like some mighty mouse who lifts his finger to the Almighty Infinite God and says, "Thus far and no further shalt Thou go." Blasphemy! And unfortunately many Christians cry with the humanists, "I am the master of my fate and the captain of my soul."

This is not the biblical picture. According to Scripture, God controls everything from the mightiest galaxy to the most infinitesimal atom. He controls the angels in heaven, the inhabitants of earth, and the kings and fortunes of nations. He raises them up and casts them down. He brings one to power and then removes it by a stroke of His hand. The Bible says, "The king's heart is in the hand of the LORD, as the rivers of water: he turneth it whithersoever he will" (Prov. 21:1). God sets up nations and sets the basest of men to rule over them. God controls planets and nations as well as the dumb beasts of earth. He said that before the cock would crow twice, Peter would deny Him thrice—and it happened! (Mark 14:30).

We see that God even controls what people call fortuitous events, because in God's economy there is nothing called luck, chance, or fate. The living God controls all things. Proverbs 16:33 says, "The lot is cast into the lap; but the whole disposing thereof is of the Lord." In 1 Samuel 14:42 when they cast lots, the lot fell on Jonathan because God controlled the casting of the lot. In the Book of Jonah, the lot fell on Jonah. In Acts 1:24–26 after the disciples prayed, they said, "Thou, Lord, which knowest the hearts of all men, shew whether of these two thou hast chosen. . . . And they gave forth their lots; and the lot fell upon Matthias." People suppose that lightning is an uncontrolled happenstance, a freak of nature, an accident. But the Bible says, "[God] covers his hands with the lightning, and commands it to strike the mark" (Job 36:32 RSV).

How about an event as fortuitous as shooting an arrow at random? The prophet said, "If thou [Ahab] return at all in peace, the Lord hath not spoken by me." And then a soldier took up his bow and shot an arrow into the air and smote the king of Israel between the joints of his armor (1 Kings 22:28, 34). God is in control of all things in this world. The tiniest events of our lives are in His hands. Even our days are numbered. As Job 14:5 says, "Seeing his days are determined, the number of his months are with thee, thou hast appointed his bounds that he cannot pass."

The Bible clearly points out that God controls the spirits of all those whom He has created. As I have stated, "the king's heart is in the hand of Jehovah as the rivers of water. He turneth it whithersoever He will." A person's goings are established by Jehovah.

God demonstrated His tremendous power in Egypt when He sent an angel to destroy the firstborn in every house of the Egyptians. And lest the Egyptians rise up and slay all the Jews, God showed His power by saying, "But against any of the children of Israel shall not a dog move his tongue, against man or beast: that ye may know how that the LORD doth put a difference between the Egyptians and Israel" (Exod. 11:7).

God controls the free acts of men. "For it is God which worketh in you both to will and to do of his good pleasure" (Phil. 2:13). Jehovah gave the people favor in the sight of the Egyptians so that they let them leave to worship their God. God further showed He was in control when He caused the Egyptians not to retaliate against the Jews, but so worked in their hearts that they lent the Israelites their gold and silver and precious stones (Exod. 12:35–36).

God's sovereignty was again displayed when the Israelites lived in the land of Canaan among a hostile people whose land they had taken and who wanted to take it back again. But God, showing His mighty control over people's hearts, arranged it so that the Canaanites would not even so much as desire the land while the men were gone to worship in Jerusalem. So three times a year, year after year, century after century, every able-bodied man in Palestine left his home open to the Hittite, the Canaanite, and the Amorite and went to Jerusalem. God so controlled their hearts that they could not so much as even desire the land.

Some people believe God can't convert a soul unless that soul gives Him permission. I wish they would ask the apostle Paul, the great hater and despiser of Christ and His church, who while on his way to Damascus to persecute the Christians, was suddenly cast to the ground by God and converted. The Bible also says that God opened the heart of Lydia and caused her to attend to the things that were spoken by Paul (Acts 16:14). "Thy people shall be willing in the day of thy power" (Ps. 110:3).

It is only God who can change the human heart. He has determined to save His elect and He will do exactly that. "All that the Father giveth me shall come to me. . . . No man can come to me, except the Father which hath sent me draw him" (John 6:37, 44). But after the example of Lucifer and Adam, sinful man still throws his autocratic will into the face of God. But hear the reply of the Almighty: "So then it is not of him that willeth, nor of him that runneth, but of God that sheweth mercy. . . . Therefore hath he mercy on whom he will have mercy, and whom he will he hardeneth" (Rom. 9:16, 18). Over and against the constant and repeated invitation to come to Christ, there needs to be set forth the balance of the divine sovereignty. Though the outward commandments of Christ may be flaunted, ignored, despised, and disobeyed, the secret counsel of Jehovah is coming to pass, and He will make the very wrath of humankind to praise Him.

There is no individual or group who could oppose, frustrate, or limit any purpose of God. The Scripture says that when all the Gentiles, together with the Jews and their rulers, set themselves to oppose God and His Christ, God "that sitteth in the heavens shall laugh: the Lord shall have them in derision" (Ps. 2:4). God is God and not man, and He does whatever He pleases in this earth, and there is no one that can speak against Him!

Is there unrighteousness then with God? God forbid. For what does God do? He looks down upon humankind and sees that every one of us has sinned and transgressed His law. "There is none righteous, no, not one. . . . They are together become unprofitable" (Rom. 3:10, 12). "The heart is deceitful above all things, and desperately wicked: who can know it? I the Lord search the heart" (Jer. 17:9–10). Therefore, God would be absolutely just if He brought a flood and once again inundated the earth. God would not be unrighteous; He would merely be a judge passing a just sentence upon wicked people. But God in His great mercy condescended to extend grace to a vast multitude whom no one can number and sent His Son to redeem those whom the Father has given Him. Furthermore, God's purposes for each always will be done.

This is seen in the story of Joseph, whose foolish and prejudiced father acted according to his own nature and gave him a coat of many colors and other preferential tokens. The foolish boy boasted to his brothers; and the brothers, according to their own evil natures, were jealous and sold him into slavery. The slave traders, according to their own greed and evil nature, bought him. Potiphar, out of a desire for gain in his household, took and made him a servant in his house. Potiphar's wife, out of lust and lasciviousness, sought to seduce him and, when he refused, had him cast into prison. But Joseph was raised up to be prime minister of Egypt; and when his brethren came for food, he said, "You meant evil against me; but God meant it for good" (Gen. 50:20 RSV).

God overrules and permits the evil acts of people so that His grace will infallibly be extended to those for whom it is ordained. His justice will inevitably come upon those who reject His Son; that is, those who are fitted for destruction. And God's glory will be manifested. Charles Spurgeon said that they would have a God who enters into His workroom and creates the universe and a God who enters into the almonry to bestow His alms. They would have a God who upholds the pillars of the earth, but when God would enter into His throne chair, then the world would gnash its teeth and shake its head and fist against God. But you and I know that the only God there is, is the God who is sovereign Lord of heaven and earth, the God who will do all of His pleasure and whose purposes will come to pass.

If you are a Christian you can say, "Thanks be unto God that the sovereign Ruler of heaven and earth is my gracious Savior." If you are not, then my friend, quickly repent of your sins and turn unto Him who says, "Him that cometh to me I will in no wise cast out" (John 6:37). Receive His mercy while there is still time. For He says, "I kill, and I make alive; I wound, and I heal; neither is there any that can deliver out of my hand" (Deut. 32:39).

Father, may we go forth into Your world knowing that You are the sovereign Ruler of every blade of grass. From the atoms in the smallest insect, to the stars that move in their courses, You are the sovereign God. O God, may none of us be guilty of the most grievous sin of rejecting Your grace, mercy, free forgiveness, and gracious gift of life eternal given to those who trust in Christ. For indeed every one of us shall one day come to Jesus Christ as Savior in this world, or as Judge in that one which is to come. *Amen.*

Does Man
Have Free Will?

If the Son therefore shall make you free, ye shall be free indeed.

John 8:36

Does man have free will? I think most recognize this to be one of the deepest subjects to have ever occupied the minds of the world's greatest thinkers. Theologians as well as philosophers have given themselves to this great enigma: Do we really have free will? Or are we merely puppets moved around by the forces of fate? It seems to be a contradiction that an all-sovereign God and a free creature could exist in the same universe. It would seem that if humanity is free, then God does not control *all* things.

First of all, to ask if man has a free will is to put the question in an improper form. It's more accurate to talk about a free agent or free soul, because the will of man never acts independently from the rest of his faculties. Man's will isn't some sort of internal gyroscope moving and turning any way

it pleases. Rather, it is an integral part of the human being—
the human soul.

What is the soul of man? Man's soul consists of intellect,
emotions, and volition or, more simply, mind, heart, and will.
Therefore, when we decide or will an action, it comes first
from the mind. Then, because we have some knowledge, we
get a feeling—human affections and appetites come into play.

These two then act on any given issue and tell the will what
to do. The will, *without exception*, does what the mind and
heart tell it to do. Man's will, therefore, never acts contrarily
to the mind and heart.

The second problem with the question, Does man have
free will? is one of semantics. What exactly do we mean by
free will? Do we mean, Do we have the ability to choose whatever we *want* to do? The answer is, Yes, we do! This is an
inalienable contribution of God to the human soul—that we
always and *only* do what we please. We are self-motivating
agents. We can originate action and choose whatever we
please on any given occasion.

Dr. John Gerstner writes that it is impossible to force the
will of man. To have a forced free will would be contrary to
the meaning of the word. He illustrates this by saying that if
he could place a book in your hands, point a gun to your
temple, and say, "You will read this book or I'll splatter your
brains all over the wall!" that would still not force your will,
because you would then come to the place of making a decision. Your mind would feed to your consciousness certain
facts, emotions, and affections as to how much you loved or
didn't love life. Quite likely you would come to the decision
to read the book!

Under other circumstances, with things more significant
than merely reading a book, there have been Christians who
have come to other conclusions. In effect, Nero said to millions of Christians, "You will renounce Jesus Christ and blas-
pheme His name, or you will wish someone would blow out
your brains. You will be peeled, boiled, fed to lions, and put in

sacks with snakes and vipers." Faced with such a choice, hundreds of thousands of Christians made a decision! Their minds fed them certain facts about this life and eternity, and most thought it was better to lose this life and gain eternity than to gain a few more years on earth and lose eternal life. Their affections went out to Jesus Christ, whom they loved more than life itself. Their decision was, "Bring on the lions!" But that was their choice! It wasn't forced! Without exception, people do whatever they please in light of the facts and feelings involved.

I said that we are free in every case to do whatever we want to do. But it doesn't necessarily follow that we are free to do what we *ought* to do! Now, what ought we to do? We ought to love God, repent of our sins, by faith embrace Jesus Christ. We ought to love the commandments of God, desire a holy life, love purity, holiness, righteousness. We ought to strive for all these things. But the Bible makes it clear that we are not free to do what we ought to do.

The Bible tells us that God made humankind—Adam and Eve—and gave them the power of contrary choice. He also gave them the ability to do that which was good, to do what they ought to. And they ought to have obeyed God and kept the commandments He gave them! Notice: They had the ability to do good as well as evil. This was humanity in a state of innocence, their first state, and without the experience of evil until they made that first fatal choice.

The Bible describes humanity's second state as being in sin. Because Adam sinned, he plunged the whole human race into sin and death in sin, which means all of us are born with his fallen nature. After first shattering and marring the image of God, Adam then brought forth creatures in his own fallen image. Some people believe humanity is born in the same condition as was Adam. This is not true. Adam was created in innocence; thereafter, all humans were born in sin. Adam was created free; we are born in bondage to sin.

The Bible describes man in sin as the natural man with a natural desire to sin. This doesn't mean we go around robbing banks! This means that whatever we do is sin. The Bible says that the plowing of the wicked is sin (Prov. 21:4). When he goes out and works at a job, it is sin. When he eats his dinner, it is sin because he's getting strength to continue his rebellion against God. In his natural state of sin, man's heart, emotions, mind, motives, ends, goals, everything is contrary to God.

The things the natural man does may be good in themselves. We may give a million dollars to charity, but we do it for the wrong reasons and the wrong motives—perhaps to get a deduction on our income tax or to get the praise of men. Jesus said "they loved the praise of men more than the praise of God" (John 12:43). We often have a false idea that in some way we're going to buy ourselves some real estate in heaven. The Bible says, "They that are in the flesh cannot please God" (Rom. 8:8). Therefore, it is impossible for the natural man to do good things without first knowing Christ, without first being born anew of the Spirit, redeemed.

The Bible also says that the natural man is at enmity against God; that he is not subject to the law of God, neither indeed can he be (Rom. 8:7). The Bible says that man is dead in his sins (Eph. 2:1, 5); he loves unrighteousness rather than righteousness; he is bound to his sin (John 3:19, 8:34).

The question now is, Does the natural man have the freedom to choose to do good, to choose Jesus Christ, to come to God? The answer is unequivocally, No!

Many Protestants talk about the natural man as if he had the power to simply cease being unrighteous and ungodly and start being godly! This was a Romanist teaching and not that of Luther or the other Reformers. One of Luther's greatest books was on *The Bondage of the Will*. It was Erasmus, the religious humanist, who wrote on the *freedom* of the will. Luther said that man was bound in sin and controlled by his own passions and desires and could not cease from these to do good. Experientially, Luther knew this to be his own condition. Jesus taught the same thing. He said, "Ye were the servants of sin.

Henceforth I call you no longer servants but friends" (see John 15:15). Jesus also said, "Whosoever committeth sin is the servant of sin" (John 8:34). It's interesting to note that Martin Luther called himself Martin Eleutheros (Martin the free). He had been the bondslave of sin, shackled by his passions and desires, but he met Christ and was set free.

Jesus said, "If the Son therefore shall make you free, ye shall be free indeed" (John 8:36), and "Ye shall know the truth, and the truth shall make you free" (John 8:32). The scribes and Pharisees, however, didn't like this. "We are Abraham's seed," they said. "We have never been in bondage to anyone." Then Jesus said, "Whosoever committeth sin is the servant of sin" (John 8:34). Iniquity and unrighteousness control the natural man's life, and he does what they tell him to do. But if the Son shall make you free, ye shall be free indeed! Consider the implication of that—if the Son shall make you free, you shall be free!

In his natural state, man is a bondslave to sin. A bondslave thinks he can do whatever he wants, but he always chooses to do the wrong thing. Place a Bible and a bottle before an alcoholic. He's free to do whatever he wants; the trouble is we know what he always wants! Invite a dope addict to a heroin party or a prayer meeting; he's free to do whatever he wants, but the problem is *what* he wants! Give a box of chocolates to a glutton; he's free to eat them or not—but is he really free? No! He's controlled by his appetite. He's bound and therefore the servant of his own emotions, affections, desires, and passions.

Let me point out that he could choose to eliminate any one of these things, but he could not choose to make himself holy. Even if he got rid of his alcohol, dope, or gluttony, he would still be an unholy sinner, incapable of choosing Jesus Christ. Why is he in this condition? His mind and heart are darkened by sin. They deceive him. He is at enmity with God.

Why is it when the natural man looks at Jesus Christ, the One who is altogether lovely, that there is nothing about Him that makes him desire Him? It's because his heart and mind give him the wrong message. He chooses not to repent and yield his life to Jesus Christ. Such a person is not free. That person is bound and in a *state of sin*.

However, when the natural man receives Jesus Christ into his heart as Savior and Lord, he is regenerated, made new, and is in a *state of grace*. He is now able to do good. Because he has God's grace, he will gain victory in his life and finally come to a *state of glory*. In a state of glory (the redeemed state of man in heaven), he has been sealed by God and is now able to do only good.

The biblical teaching about man is this: First, he was in the *state of innocence*—able to do good, able to sin. Second, in the *state of sin* (his fallen nature), he is able only to sin. He is unable to change his moral nature, incapable of lifting himself up into holiness. Third, in the *state of grace*, he can do both. And fourth, in the *state of glory*, he will be sealed to do only that which is good.

If you've never received Jesus Christ, then I urge you to examine yourself and see your utter helplessness, your total inability to suppose yourself to do anything but that which is displeasing to God. May you be enabled by His grace to cry out to the Son of Glory to set you free—that you may be free indeed!

> Long my imprisoned spirit lay
> Fast bound in sin and nature's night.
> Thine eye diffused a quick'ning ray;
> I woke—the dungeon flamed with light!
> My chains fell off, my heart was free,
> I rose, went forth, and followed thee.
>
> Charles Wesley

Lord Jesus, we thank You that You have made those that trust in You free. That You have made us kings and heirs of Your kingdom. That You have delivered us from the bondage of sin and declared that sin shall no longer have dominion over us. Father, I pray for those who are still in the bondage of their own making. A bondage which ties, binds, and draws them downward ever into deeper sin. I pray, Father, that You will deliver them from these shackles and set the prisoners free. May they come out of their bondage, darkness, and sin to the One who can make them free—to Christ, the great Emancipator from sin. *Amen.*

3

Predestination

And we know that all things work together for good to them that love God, to them who are the called according to his purpose. For whom he did foreknow, he also did predestinate to be conformed to the image of his Son, that he might be the firstborn among many brethren. Moreover whom he did predestinate, them he also called: and whom he called, them he also justified: and whom he justified, them he also glorified.

Romans 8:28–30

I had a brief discourse with a friend recently during which I mentioned predestination. This prompted an outburst concerning why the doctrine of predestination was contrary to all manner of Christian principles, ethics, and motives. Unfortunately, I did not have time to discuss the matter further with the gentleman, but I think he is typical of many people today, both in and out of the church, who would find the doctrine of predestination to be somewhat alien. You would think that one were a setter-forth of strange doctrines, as the apostle Paul was accused of being, when you mention the doctrine of predestination—as if this were something totally foreign and alien to Christianity. Truly this doctrine has fallen on bad times in our day.

Why is this? The great A. A. Hodge, professor at Princeton, said that this is due, in a large measure, to the inattention that is paid to it in the churches and to the general prevalence of a natural, though unfounded and ignorant, prejudice against it. I think it is true that there is a natural prejudice on the part of people against this doctrine, as there is to all of the doctrines of grace, and since at this point the sovereign grace of God reaches its apex, that prejudice becomes most obvious here.

B. B. Warfield, also at Princeton, said in answer to the question of why people in this particular time are so opposed to this doctrine, "Consider the pride of man, his assertion of freedom, his boast of power, his refusal to acknowledge the sway of any other's will. Consider the ingrained confidence of the sinner in his own fundamentally good nature." How true this is. As I have talked to thousands of people, I find that most of them are basically convinced that at their heart and in their core, they are basically good. Well, that wasn't what Jesus said about the heart, was it? Some of these people say, "Oh, I believe that Jesus is the Master Teacher." Jesus said that we are, every one of us, sinners in our hearts, "for out of the heart proceed evil thoughts, murders, adulteries, fornications, thefts, false witness, blasphemies" (Matt. 15:19). The Bible says, "The heart is deceitful above all things, and desperately wicked: who can know it? I the Lord search the heart" (Jer. 17:9–10). Yet the unregenerate person, the non-Christian, has an ingrained confidence in his or her fundamentally good nature. There is no such thing, we are told, as a bad boy. Well, how many times have we heard that? But that is not what the Scripture says. The Scripture says, "There is none that doeth good, no, not one" (Ps. 53:3)—boy or man, girl or woman, Christian or non-Christian—there is none good, no, not one. The whole class has flunked because of man's ingrained confidence in his full ability to perform all

that can be justly demanded of him. Warfield says that particularly at this time, when man, through science, has made
such spectacular advances in power over nature and is so filled
with pride of accomplishment, he finds it particularly diffi-
cult to humble himself beneath the mighty hand of God. We
must come to the place of realizing that we are not only guilty
and polluted, but absolutely helpless and hopeless. There is
nothing we can do to prepare ourselves, for our salvation is
entirely in the hands of God. That is why Dr. L. Boettner
says that it is almost impossible to convince the unregenerate heart of this doctrine. Let me say that again: It is almost
impossible to convince the unregenerate heart (the unsaved
person, the unbeliever) of this doctrine. The natural man, in
his natural unregenerate state, rises up in revolt against it.
And so, being the pinnacle of sovereign grace, it is a touch-
stone by which people's characters are revealed, as to whether
they are truly submissive to Christ and His Word. In studying it, your heart will be revealed to you this hour. You will
never be the same. Some of you will hate the thought of predestination; some will love and cherish it. But keep in mind,
it is practically impossible to convince the unregenerate mind
of this doctrine.

That this should be looked upon as an alien doctrine today
is even stranger when we take a brief historical review. This
doctrine was set forth very plainly in the early church by Saint
Augustine, so much that it held sway over the church for most
of the early centuries until the church finally sank into apostasy. It was revived again by Martin Luther, who was a firm
believer in the doctrine of predestination. John Calvin of
Geneva was also a firm believer and set it forth with such
cogency and power that it has even taken on his name in some
circles as if he had invented it, which of course is far from the
truth. He simply stated it with great clarity. It was held also
by Melanchthon, by Zwingli, by John Knox, and by Cran-
mer in England. Without exception, all of the Reformers of
the Protestant Reformation were firm believers in the doc-

trine of predestination. It was, says Hastings, the historian, "the very Hercules might of the Protestant Reformation whereby the Reformers took the salvation of the human soul out of the hands of the pope and put it firmly in the hands of God." Now is it not strange that the descendants of these Reformers, who claim to believe their doctrines, so frequently vehemently deny this, which they held to be a cardinal teaching of the Scriptures? All Protestant churches that came into being out of the Reformation hold to this doctrine in their creeds. The most moral people that the world has ever seen have been believers in this doctrine. The Presbyterians and the Reformed of Holland and Switzerland and Germany, the Anglicans, the Huguenots, the Covenanters, the Puritans, the Pietists of Germany, the Pilgrims of America, were all firm believers in this great doctrine of predestination.

The makers of civil liberty, such as John Calvin; the virtual founder of democracy, William of Orange; Cromwell; and the Presbyterian and Congregational founders of the government of this nation were all believers in this great doctrine. Pioneer provisions for universal education sprang from the Scottish parochial school, which was built upon this doctrine. The New England College was founded upon this great teaching as well. Dr. L. Boettner said that the patriots, free-state makers, martyrs, and missionaries of the modern era have been overwhelmingly believers in the doctrine of predestination.

Therefore, I would have you reconsider whatever prejudice you may have against this doctrine in the light of some of these facts of history. What I would urge would be a calm, careful study of the matter. I am sure that what you will obtain in one chapter like this would not be sufficient, and I would urge you to make a further study of it. There are many books dealing with the subject. I would encourage you to study them. Adapting the words of Alexander Pope, we might say that a little predestination is a dangerous thing, so drink deeply from the sacred spring or drink not at all.

The reason people today are opposed to it is because they will have God to be anything but God. He can be a cosmic psychiatrist, a helpful shepherd, a leader, a teacher, anything at all—only not God. For a very simple reason—they want to be God themselves. This has always been the essence of sin—that man wants to be God—from the very time that Lucifer said, "I will be like the most High" (Isa. 14:14). So Adam said to God, "God, you keep your hands off my life. I'm going to run it my way" (see Gen. 3). Oh, it's not that we desire so much to bind the influences of the Pleiades or manipulate Orion, it's that we want to be the God of our own lives. We want to be the captains of our fates and the masters of our souls. This mastery we do not want to give up to God or anyone else.

But what about the Scriptures? I am tempted to ask sometimes of people who say they do not believe in this doctrine, "Do you believe in the Bible?" One unquestionable thing is that the Scriptures are filled with this teaching. Simply to write out the passages in the Scripture that deal with predestination, election, the efficacious calling of God's Spirit of people unto salvation, foreordination, God's sovereignty over all phases of the world, would take more space than we have in this entire chapter. That you might see that this doctrine is plainly taught in the Scripture, let us look at a few. That there are a group of people in the Bible known as the *elect*—those that are chosen of God—is clear from such passages as these: "Except those days [the last days] should be shortened, there should no flesh be saved: but for the elect's sake those days shall be shortened." "For there shall arise false Christs, and false prophets, and shall shew great signs and wonders; insomuch that, if it were possible, they shall deceive the very elect." "And [God] shall send his angels with a great sound of a trumpet, and they shall gather together his elect from the four winds" (Matt. 24:22, 24, 31). "Who shall lay any thing to the charge of God's elect? It is God that justifieth. Who is he that condemneth?" (Rom. 8:33–34). Christ said that we should rejoice because our names are written in the Lamb's book of life (Luke 10:20; Rev. 21:27), written from the foundation of the earth. Said Paul, "Therefore I endure all things for the elect's sakes" (2 Tim. 2:10). "Paul, a servant of God, and an apostle of Jesus Christ, according to the faith of God's elect" (Titus 1:1). "Knowing, brethren beloved, your election of God" (1 Thess. 1:4). We can know that we are elect. If we have come to Christ and have been regenerated and redeemed, we may know that we are elect because we would never come otherwise.

Also we read of God's "having predestinated us unto the adoption of children by Jesus Christ to himself, according to the good pleasure of his will. . . . In whom also we have obtained an inheritance, being predestinated according to the purpose of him who worketh all things after the counsel of his own will" (Eph. 1:5, 11).

Romans 8:30 tells us that "Moreover whom he did predestinate, them he also called: and whom he called, them he also justified: and whom he justified, them he also glorified." We see the "golden chain" that takes our salvation from eternity past to eternity future and is bound up in the predestinating love and will of God.

When Jesus had gone into Bethsaida, Capernaum, and various towns and preached, and His preaching had been rejected, what did He do? Did He sit down by the edge of the road and say, "Oh, Father, I'm so miserable! They have all rejected my preaching. I did the best I could, but they just wouldn't hearken unto me. They just wouldn't respond! Oh, Lord, I surely wish that they would respond. I'm so sad." Is that what He did? Read His words in Matthew 11:25–26. Jesus at that time lifted up His eyes to heaven and said, "I thank thee, O Father, Lord of heaven and earth, because thou hast hid these things from the wise and prudent, and hast revealed them unto babes." Why? Why has God done this? "Even so, Father: for so it seemed good in thy sight."

Now, since this is just a sampling of many, many passages that mention this doctrine, what does it actually mean? What is it saying? Charles Spurgeon, considered by many to be the most famous and outstanding preacher of all times, said that in a world of fallen men, where all of them have rebelled against God and gone the way of their own sin, have turned their backs upon Him, where none will seek after God, for there is none that seeketh after God, no, not one, what good is a *whosoever will* in a world where *everybody won't?* Man inevitably refuses to come to God, though God would extend His arms all day long. "All day long I have stretched forth my hands unto a disobedient and gainsaying people" (Rom. 10:21), saying, "Why will ye not come? Why will ye die? And you would not" (see John 5:40).

There are only two things anyone is going to get from God: one is justice. God must be just with everyone. The judge of the earth must do rightly (see Ps. 98:9). It is incumbent upon God to be just to everyone. He cannot be unfair or unjust.

The other thing that we can get is mercy or grace. Someone said to me one time, "Well, that's not fair." That's right! It isn't! Salvation isn't fair. If you have not learned that by now, you haven't learned much of anything about Christianity. It isn't fair. Fair means just, and just means you get exactly what you deserve depending upon what you have done in light of what you have known. If we get what we deserve depending upon what we've done, we are going to get it right in the neck because we've all done wrong. Thank God that grace is not fair!

Now it is not unfair in the sense that it is below fair. But it is *super*fair, it is mercy, it is beyond and above fairness. If you sell a piece of property that is worth a thousand dollars, and the buyer cheats you and only gives you five hundred dollars, that is not fair. But suppose the buyer gives you five hundred thousand dollars for a piece of property that is evidently worth only a thousand. That is not fair; that is better than fair. Grace is better than fair.

God doesn't have to give grace or mercy to anyone. He said, "I will have mercy on whom I will have mercy" (Rom. 9:15). When a governor forgives or pardons some criminal in the penitentiary, it doesn't mean that he has to pardon every criminal in every penitentiary in the state. That is an executive privilege of a sovereign. He may extend it or withhold it as he sees fit. God looks down upon a fallen world and decides to extend mercy and to freely forgive a person who condignly deserves to be punished for his sins. Therefore God extends to that person mercy. Charles Spurgeon asked if there was anything wrong with that. And so I ask you, Is there anything wrong with God extending mercy and freely pardoning and forgiving someone who doesn't deserve it at all? "Is it not lawful for me to do what I will with mine own?" (Matt. 20:15) said Christ when He extended mercy to someone. No, there is nothing wrong with that. According to Spurgeon, then is it not all right that God should *decide* to do that yesterday and then *do* it today? Or decide to do it last week and then do it today? Or last month or year or century or before the foundation of the world? And that, my friends, is election or predestination: that God looked down from all eternity upon a world of sinners and decided to extend mercy to a vast number of people whom no one can number; and that in their appointed time He extended that mercy, not because of anything foreseen in them, but entirely and totally because of what God is—the God of all grace. So much for the statement of the doctrine.

Many objections have been raised against this. One is, "Well, why doesn't God save everyone?" There are some things that are revealed; and the things that are revealed belong unto the children of men, and the things that are not revealed belong unto God (Deut. 29:29). God has not been pleased to reveal to us everything. He has not revealed to us fully why He has not chosen everyone. But it is for reasons that seem good in His sight. Why did Jesus say that He had withheld this grace? Notice His words again, "I thank thee,

O Father, Lord of heaven and earth, that thou hast hid these things from the wise and prudent, and hast revealed them unto babes." Why? "Even so, Father; for so it seemed good in thy sight" (Luke 10:21). Some of you won't like that. This is the place where you find whether or not you are willing to be submissive to God—not to an arbitrary pagan deity, but to a God infinitely wise, infinitely gracious, infinitely just, infinitely holy. For reasons that seem good to Him, He has extended grace to some and withheld it from others.

The Bible gives us some clues. One thing we can know— what is *not* the reason why it is extended to those of us to whom it has been extended. He didn't extend it to us because we are better than anyone else, or nobler than anyone else, or wiser or smarter or holier than anyone else. Rather, the Bible says in 1 Corinthians 1:26–29, 31, "For ye see your calling, brethren, how that not many wise men after the flesh, not many mighty, not many noble, are called. But God hath chosen the foolish things of the world to confound the wise; and God hath chosen the weak things of the world to confound the things which are mighty; and base things of the world, and things which are despised, hath God chosen, yea, and things which are not, to bring to nought things that are: that no flesh should glory in his presence." So the fact that I know that I am one of God's elect gives me no grounds for boasting, because God specifically tells me that He has chosen the junk of this world. There is no place for boasting. "He that glorieth, let him glory in the Lord" (v. 31).

Salvation is not by works or human merit, lest anyone should boast. We have nothing to boast about. We also may derive from the Scripture this realization: that God has created the world for His own glory and not simply for our pleasure. God is glorified because He is a glorious Being. The many facets of God's character, like a magnificent diamond, are glorious; and to be glorified, they simply must be seen. Thus in the salvation of the redeemed, the glorious aspects of God's mercy, grace, compassion, long-suffering, kindness, and love are revealed and God is glorified. But in the just condemnation of the wicked, the glorious aspects of God's justice, holiness, and righteousness are manifested; and God is also glorified. Now for us, who see all of this with the jaundiced eyes of sinners, we find that hard to understand. But an angel, who is without sin, would find no difficulty with it at all. God is just and holy and righteous and has a natural indignation and hatred of sin because sin is inherently evil. When these qualities are manifested in the just condemnation of sinners, God in His justice is glorified in the same way that a judge is glorified when he justly condemns a wicked criminal. Therefore, both in the electing of some and the passing by of others, God is glorified.

Others have raised this objection, "Why, this is fatalism!" This simply reveals how little they know about predestination or how little they know about fatalism. If they understood both of these properly, they would know that predestination is the only genuine alternative to fatalism. This is important. Fatalism allows no place for any sort of freedom for humankind. Where the Bible teaches that the natural, unsaved, unregenerate man is dead and bound in his sins and therefore cannot do the things that he *ought*, such as repenting and living a holy life, it also teaches that all people whether in the state of innocence, sin, grace, or glory, are always free to do what they *want*. Let me state that again. Though man in his natural, unregenerate state is bound in sin and cannot do what he *ought*, all people are always free to do what they *want* (Acts 26:18). Because they are free to do whatever they please, they are responsible for whatever they do. Therefore, the liberty and contingency of second causes are maintained, and not destroyed as they are in fatalism.

Some people suppose that by accepting the doctrine of chance they will avoid this problem. But all you have to do is read cursorily in the philosophy of science to know that chance is absolutely deterministic. The only difference between chance and fatalism is that in fatalism you are held by some impersonal force that controls everything; in chance, you are given over into the hands of some sort of impersonal machine which is either going to chop you up or bring you out on top, but is an impersonal, unthinking force. Whereas, the Bible would put us into the hands of an all-knowing, all-loving Father, a personal Being. There is a vast gulf of difference between fatalism and predestination. This is even more obvious as Jesus said, "For the tree is known by its fruit" (Matt. 12:33). Look at the Muslim world where fatalism has been its teaching for thirteen hundred years. There you see nations that have been plunged into stagnation and poverty. Then look to the lands of the doctrine of predestination—Switzerland, Holland, Germany, England, Scotland, America—and you see nations that have had the greatest of progress. The difference is so obvious that the most cursory examination would reveal it.

Some object that predestination destroys any sort of motivation. This is because people have the idea that in order to be motivated to do anything, what is done must be unknown and uncertain. But this is not true. And a little reflection will show that regardless of what you believe about predestination, if you believe in God at all, you believe in an omniscient Being who knows all things. "Known unto God are all his works from the beginning of the world," Acts 15:18 says. God knows everything. Now, if you have a God that simply knows everything, that knowledge renders every future event certain. May I point out why? A hundred million years ago, did God know that you would be reading this book at this hour? You say, "Of course, God knew everything." He knew that a hundred million years ago. If you don't believe that, you don't believe in God. Everybody who believes in God knows that one of the attributes of God is omniscience. If God didn't know that and He just learned it today because He saw you here, then God just learned something and thus God would not be immutable or unchangeable. He would have just changed; He just grew in His knowledge. Thus He is destroyed as God. If God, a hundred million years ago, knew that you were going to be reading this book at this hour, is there any possibility that you would not now be reading it? Of course not! His knowledge rendered that fact absolutely certain. You know that. At the same time, you know that you picked up this book by your own free will because you are free to do what you please to do. Now this is a mystery we cannot comprehend, how God has ordained all things to work together as people please and yet God overrules and works everything according to His will. "For it is God which worketh in you both to will and to do of his good pleasure" (Phil. 2:13).

So you see that regardless of what you believe about predestination, if you simply believe in God, an omniscient God, every future act is rendered certain. But the fact that something is certain doesn't mean that you are not free. That God will always act in a righteous manner is absolutely certain. There is no question about that. He cannot act in any other way, and yet there is no being so free as God. Therefore the doctrine of predestination, because it renders future events certain, does not take away the liberty of secondary causes; nor does it mean that people are not free to do what they want.

Some people say, "Why should I pray?" For example, when you pray that God would convert some non-Christian friend or relative, are you not praying that God would do the very thing that we are talking about? If God can't do this, if God cannot convert people, if it is not God who saves people, if all we can do is present facts and hope that people will respond, then there is no sense in really praying to God at all. One of the first rules of salesmanship is to go to the person who has the power to make the decision. So quit getting on your knees to God and go kneel down before the man and pray to him to be saved. He has the final decision, if you don't believe in predestination. But we pray always as if God had the ability to convert the soul just as He did the apostle Paul (Acts 9:1–20).

"Why should we witness and why should we preach?" The reason people ask this is because they do not understand that God doesn't foreordain simply the ends, but He also foreordains the means. If He has foreordained that somebody would be converted, He has also foreordained that somebody would share the gospel and would pray for him or her. That person in turn would have been converted prior to that—the continuous praying and converting would have reached all the way back to the beginning of the world. God never foreordains ends without also foreordaining means.

The doctrine of election is full of great consolation, and there are great practical benefits to holding it and understanding it. The Thirty-nine Articles of the Church of England, in its seventeenth article, says, "The godly consideration of Predestination, and our Election in Christ, is full of sweet, pleasant, and unspeakable comfort to godly persons." Notice that it is a comfort "to godly persons." But if you are not godly, it is not full of comfort to you. It is full of comfort because it shows that salvation is all of grace. Keep in mind that the Bible never says that anyone is predestined to hell. The word is only used of heaven, grace, and glory. But you say, "If God predestinates some to heaven, and if He passes by others, isn't He predestinating them to hell?" No, that is not the case, because this supposes that these people are neutral and are not going anyplace by themselves. The whole world is rushing headlong into wickedness and sin, and thus into condemnation and hell.

Here are five people who are planning to hold up a bank. They are friends of mine. I find out about it and I plead with them. I beg them not to do it. Finally they push me out of the way and they start out. I tackle one of the men and wrestle him to the ground. The others go ahead and rob the bank. A guard is killed, they are captured, convicted, sentenced to the electric chair, and die. The one man who was not involved in the robbery goes free. Now I ask you this question: Whose fault was it that these other men died? Did I make them hold

up the bank? Did I encourage them to do it? Did I cause them
to do it? Did I urge them to do it? Or did I not plead with
them not to do it? Was it not their own free choice of their
own sinful hearts, their own cupidity, their own lust for
money, that caused them to do it? They had nobody to blame
but themselves. Now this other man who is walking around
free—can he say, "Because my heart is so good, I am a free
man"? The only reason that he is free is because of me,
because I restrained him. So those who go to hell have no one
to blame but themselves. Those who go to heaven have no
one to praise but Jesus Christ. Thus we see that salvation is
all of grace, from its beginning to its end. It is all of God. He
is the one that seeks us and draws us unto Himself.

This doctrine gives great security and courage to those
who believe it. For those for whom God is far away and may
only now and then be involved in the activities of this life,
life is full of fear and danger. But those that live and move in
God and know that He sovereignly controls every atom of
this universe, these people are filled with good courage and
confidence. Predestination extinguishes fear, and it is interesting to note that those who held to it were afraid of no one.
It brings people low before God, but it lifts Him high. It
makes people strong before kings. Thus Mary Queen of Scots
could say that she feared the face of John Knox more than
ten thousand ships.

Do you know, beloved, your election in Christ? The Bible
says, "Make your calling and election sure." Christ is inviting
you to come. Predestination keeps no one out of heaven, but
it populates paradise with a multitude of people that no one
can number. Christ says, "Come to me; and him that cometh
to me, I will in no wise cast out." But of yourself, you will
never come. "There is none that seeketh after God. No, not
one." If you do not come to Christ, trust His cross, cease to
trust in your own righteousness, and put your trust in His
atoning work, you have nothing to blame but the self-righ-
teousness, pride, and love of sin in your own heart. If you do

come to Christ, it will be because God, the great and gracious Shepherd, has sought you out and brought you to Himself. The lost sheep does not find the shepherd; the shepherd finds the lost sheep.

> Hark! 'tis the Shepherd's voice I hear,
> Out in the desert dark and drear,
> Calling the sheep who've gone astray
> Far from the Shepherd's fold away.

Soli Deo Gloria!

Effectual Calling

Moreover whom he did predestinate, them he also called: and whom he called, them he also justified: and whom he justified, them he also glorified.

Romans 8:30

In the first three chapters, we have seen that God is the sovereign Ruler of the world. He does not work helter-skelter, nor does He ad-lib as He goes along day by day. Rather He laid the architectural plans for all His works before He created the world. He sovereignly controls and ordains all things that come to pass, from the greatest star to the smallest atom.

We have seen that He has done this in such a way as to leave a certain natural liberty to humankind. He created humanity with a power to do good or evil. But humankind chose evil and plunged the world into sin, bringing humanity into a state of bondage and condemnation. We find God determined not to leave humanity there, but from all eternity selected a people for Himself. The Scriptures refer to these as His elect, His chosen ones—a multitude of every tongue, kindred, nation, and tribe under the sun; a multitude no one can number (see Mark 13:20, 27). These God determined to save. These are His sheep, the predestinated ones for whom Paul bore all things and for whom the days of tribulation will be shortened. These are the ones who will hear and understand His voice and will follow Him because they know God sent His Son to die and procure eternal life for them.

In this chapter, I want to consider how this redemption, which has been procured by Christ and chosen by God, is to be applied. This doctrine is called *effectual calling*. Most know what a calling is, but what is an effectual calling? *Effectual* means that which effectuates whatever it attempts to do. It is that which works, is successful, and succeeds in doing that which the author intends. This is what God means when He says, "[My word] shall not return unto me void, but it shall accomplish that which I please, and it shall prosper in the thing whereto I sent it" (Isa. 55:11). What purpose shall it accomplish? Shall it accomplish the purpose of the people that hear it? No, it shall accomplish the purpose for which God sent it. It is effectual to do His work.

The Bible speaks of both a calling that is effectual and a calling that is not. There is the outer calling, which is merely the Word unaccompanied by the Holy Spirit. When I say in the name of Jesus Christ that He declares, "Come unto me and I will give you life," that's an outward, external calling by the Word. If someone should respond to that calling, he or she would receive eternal life because God will refuse no one. "Him that cometh to me I will in no wise cast out" (John 6:37).

But there is a problem. In his fallen condition natural, unregenerate man is so bound by sin and blinded by his iniquity that he desires to have nothing to do with the Holy God because his heart is at enmity with God. "There is none that understandeth, there is none that seeketh after God" (Rom. 3:11). Every person who seeks after God will find Him. "And ye shall seek me, and find me, when ye shall search for me with all your heart" (Jer. 29:13). But there is none that seeketh after God. Why? "But the natural man receiveth not the things of the Spirit of God: for they are foolishness unto him: neither can he know them, because they are spiritually discerned" (1 Cor. 2:14). The problem is man's will, which is set against God and bound in its own sin.

Therefore, before a person comes to Christ, there must be something more than an external invitation. There must be an inward work of the Spirit of God who effectually woos and draws us to Christ so we come freely, being made willing by His grace. The ineffectual calling (the outward call) is seen in Matthew 22:14, "For many are called [by the gospel every week], but few are chosen." Keep in mind that the few is a multitude no one can number, but few compared to the vast billions of people who have lived upon earth.

The effectual or inward call is seen in Romans 8:30, "Whom he did predestinate, them he also called: and whom he called, them he also justified." Those he called, came! Unquestionably, all God's elect shall come unto Him. "All that the Father giveth me shall come to me . . ." (John 6:37). All those the Father has given unto the Son as a reward for His suffering and passion will come unto Him and He shall see His seed and be satisfied (see Isa. 53:11). So there is both an outward and an inward call.

This doctrine of effectual calling is also called *irresistible* or *efficacious grace*. The following is a succinct statement of this doctrine as contained in the Westminster Confession of Faith, which is the doctrinal standard of the Reformed world.

> All of those whom God hath predestinated unto life, and those only, He is pleased, in His appointed and accepted time, effectually to call, by His Word and Spirit, out of that state of sin and death in which they are by nature, to grace and salvation by Jesus Christ: enlightening their minds, spiritually and savingly, to understand the things of God, taking away their heart of stone, and giving unto them an heart of flesh, renewing their wills, and

by His almighty power determining them to that which is good; and effectually drawing them to Jesus Christ; yet so as they come most freely, being made willing by His grace. This effectual call is of God's free and special grace alone, not from anything at all foreseen in man, who is altogether passive therein, until, being quickened and renewed by the Holy Spirit, he is thereby enabled to answer this call, and to embrace the grace offered and conveyed in it.

This then is effectual calling. The agent is the Holy Spirit; the instrument is the Word of God; the objects of the call are unregenerate sinners, specifically those of God's elect.

In 2 Thessalonians 2:13–14 we read, "God hath from the beginning chosen you to salvation . . . whereunto he called you by our gospel, to the obtaining of the glory of our Lord Jesus Christ." And there you have the picture. Before the beginning of the world, God chose them, and having chosen them, He determined to see that they received the gift of eternal life. He is going to bring it to pass in His appointed time. The Spirit will call them by the gospel unto Christ, and they will receive that which God has given them.

Of course, there are many people who don't begin to understand the rudiments of Christianity and who suppose salvation is something earned by their own good works. But salvation is a gift—unearned, unmerited, and undeserved. It is a gift given purely by the grace and goodness of God. Now the question is, How does He give this gift? We look around and see that some people hear the gospel and embrace Jesus Christ, while others do not. Those who accept Jesus Christ into their lives are puzzled about why others, who have heard the same gospel, do not.

There are two schools of thought, or two theological systems within Protestantism, which attempt to answer this question. The first is Calvinism, which is espoused by the Presbyterian Church and many others; the second is Arminianism. Both are named after theologians, John Calvin and

Jacob Arminius. The Arminian says, "The difference is to be found in man." The Calvinist says, "The difference is to be found in God," and quotes the following Scripture to support his view: "For who maketh thee to differ from another? and what hast thou that thou didst not receive?" (1 Cor. 4:7). What causes you to differ? Yourself? What do you have that you did not receive? Do you have faith? Where did you get it? Do you have repentance? Where did you get it? Do you love God? Whence is that love? All springs from the fountain of God.

But the Arminian system says God offers eternal life to everyone, and some will believe and accept it; others will not. If this were true, then a person could say, "I have heard the gospel; I believe and accept Christ; therefore, I have eternal life. But you, my neighbor, have heard the same gospel, but because of your sinful and hard heart you've turned your back and rejected it. Therefore, you are not saved and I am." The difference is to be found in us! In a sense the person is saying, "I am better than you—more spiritual, more religious, more softhearted, less in love with sin and the world. Therefore I will cling tenaciously to something in which I can boast. If I cannot boast of my good works, I shall at least boast of my faith." The Bible says, "But he that glorieth, let him glory in the Lord" (2 Cor. 10:17).

The two basic problems with the Arminian view are found in the nature of God and the nature of man. Most people do not understand the biblical picture of the nature of man. After the fall, man died spiritually and remained in a condition from which nothing but the almighty power of God could deliver him. Failing to understand this, people suppose man can free himself from his trespasses and sin. But Jesus said to the Pharisees, "If the Son therefore shall make you free, ye shall be free indeed" (John 8:36), which is to say that before He performs this gracious act for them, they are not free indeed. Over and over the Bible says (concerning the natural man), "Who can bring a clean thing out of an unclean? not one" (Job

14:4). But some people believe man's will is strong enough to bring a clean life, a good life, a holy act of faith, out of an unclean man. Romans 5:12 says, "Wherefore, as by one man sin entered into the world, and death by sin; and so death passed upon all men, for that all have sinned." Man is dead in his trespasses and sins!

"Can the Ethiopian change his skin, or the leopard his spots? then may ye also do good, that are accustomed to do evil." "Behold, I was shapen in iniquity; and in sin did my mother conceive me." "As it is written, There is none righteous, no, not one. There is none that understandeth, there is none that seeketh after God." If the gospel consisted of no more than an invitation, then heaven indeed would be an empty place. As Spurgeon said, "What good is a 'whosoever will' in a world where everybody won't!'"

So the first problem with the Arminian view is that man is not free to do what he ought. Let me make this clear: Man is always free to do what he wants; that's why he's responsible for everything he does. But he doesn't have the power to do what he ought. He ought to love God with all his heart, strength, mind, and soul, but he cannot change his character any more than the Ethiopian can change his skin or the leopard his spots. No, he is bound in his sins and, until Christ breaks the shackles and sets the prisoner free, he will remain forever bound in his own sin.

The second problem with the Arminian viewpoint is the problem of God. They say that God offers all people the choice of eternal life; therefore, it's up to each person to decide whether to choose it or not. God, they say, is trying desperately to save everybody in the world, but it's up to us to determine whether we're going to let Him. They picture God as saying, "It is My will that everybody in the world should be saved. But, alas, in the end I must say not My will but thine be done. For thou, O man, art the sovereign Lord of this world, not I!" This is the humanist viewpoint and they like it because it elevates their own will.

Some people suppose that because God says He would that all should be saved and is not willing that any should perish, He's actively trying to save everybody in the world. This, I think, is a false view. If God were actively trying to do something and were prevented from doing it, then He would not be God.

It is also false from the multiple statements of Scripture that state that God is absolutely sovereign over all things, including the spirit, will, and heart of man (see Eph. 1:9). The Bible says, "He doeth all of His pleasure among the armies of heaven and the inhabitants of earth; He stretched forth His hand and there is none that can say unto Him, 'What doeth thou?' or turn His hand back." As Romans 9:19 says, "For who hath resisted his will?" The answer to that is nobody—no one has ever resisted the will of God. The Bible says that He will perform all of His purpose and that not one purpose of His will be restrained.

Do we have a God who is desperately trying to save everybody and is equally failing; or do we have a God who has set His purpose and fixed His heart upon His own people, His elect, whom He has chosen before the foundation of the world? The sovereign Lord God of heaven and earth is unfailingly bringing every one of them into glory!

Who is the God you worship? God could be equally just and merciful if He never saved anyone. Spurgeon said that the amazing thing is not that everybody is not saved, but that anybody is saved. There is the marvel of God's grace—the general benevolence of God; He isn't willing people into perdition or causing them to be lost—their own hearts are. God's general pleasure and favor are that He is willing for all to come. He says, "I have no pleasure in the death of the wicked . . . why will ye die?" (Ezek. 33:11). But God's secret purpose is to save those whom He has ordained from the foundation of the world. All these shall be saved. "Moreover whom he did predestinate, them he also called: and whom he called, them he also justified: and whom he justified, them he also glorified" (Rom. 8:30). So it is God the Holy Spirit who does the calling.

Remember, it is the Word of God that is the creative force of this world. Consider the physical universe for a moment. From where does the physical universe come? God said, "Let there be light" (Gen. 1:3), and a multitude of galaxies leaped into existence, flaming in the sky. By the word of God, the worlds which we see began.

Consider Lazarus. Jesus said to him, "Lazarus, come forth" (John 11:43). But Lazarus was dead; he couldn't hear Him. If Jesus had no more than an invitation to give to him, He could have knocked at that tombstone door forever. But Christ spoke the life-giving word, and that word brought Lazarus to life and caused his heart to beat and his lungs to work. Lazarus heard the voice of his Master and said in effect, "My beloved calls. I will go," having been made willing by His grace.

Consider the matter of your own physical birth. What did you have to do with it? This is a perfect example of the absolute sovereignty of God; you were not consulted in the matter! No one said, "Do you want to be sir or madam? Would you like to have black hair, blond, or perhaps no hair at all? Would you like your eyes to be brown or blue? Would you like to have white or black skin, or would red, or yellow suit you better? And where would you like to live? In Fort Lauderdale, Hong Kong, or maybe in Zaire?" Nothing of the sort! You were not consulted at all. The sovereign Lord God of heaven and earth brought you into existence without so much as a how-do-you-feel-about-it!

So it is true of our spiritual birth. God didn't consult us. God brings us to life by His own sovereign power. What is necessary for man to be reborn? Two things: God's Spirit and God's Word. That is what Jesus meant when He talked to Nicodemus. He said that a person must be born of water and the Spirit (see John 3:5). Water, in Scripture, is a frequent allusion to the Word of God. "Ye are clean through the word which I have spoken unto you" (John 15:3).

It is necessary to have the outward calling of the Word. That Word is accompanied by the inward calling of the Holy Spirit, who takes the gospel of Jesus Christ and makes it a life-creating force that quickens dead sinners from death in sin and brings them to life in Christ. The Holy Spirit takes away their darkened minds, illumines their understanding, unstops their ears, takes away their hearts of stone, gives them hearts of flesh, and renews their dead wills. After hearing the invitation, sinners say, "I will come to Thee, O Christ." Afterward they *know* it was Christ who brought them to Himself.

But what of those who are not effectually called? They hear the outward call. May I say to you again, the Word of Christ is explicit: "Him that cometh to me I will in no wise cast out" (John 6:37). You see, I can say that to you, but I know that unless the Spirit of God comes to you and changes your whole nature, you'll never come, and for one reason: You don't want to come! Would you like to know if you are one of God's elect? Come to Christ and you will know you are, because you never would have come otherwise. "Whosoever shall call upon the name of the Lord shall be saved" (Acts 2:21). When you do that, you'll know it was the Spirit of God who drew you to Himself. There is a poem that puts it thus:

> I sought the Lord, and afterward I knew
> He moved my soul to seek Him, seeking me;
> It was not I that found, O Saviour true,
> No, I was found of Thee.
>
> Author unknown

It is not the lost sheep that finds the Shepherd!

5

The Incomparable Christ

Wherefore God also hath highly exalted him, and given him a name which is above every name: that at the name of Jesus every knee should bow, of things in heaven, and things in earth, and things under the earth; and that every tongue should confess that Jesus Christ is Lord, to the glory of God the Father.

Philippians 2:9–11

Returning from a conference by plane, I found myself seated next to a young man who was a television director from Boston. As time went on, our conversation turned to the subject of religion. He mentioned the fact that he believed himself to be a Christian, that he believed in Jesus Christ; and then he said, "However, of course, that does not mean that I do not also believe all of the other religions are good and valid and that all the other founders of these religions are also great men. Of course, I do not go along with the idea that Jesus is the 'only way.'"

That brought to my mind the question so many people ask today, "Is Christ really the only way?" Is He the incomparable Christ? Is there no one with whom He can truthfully be compared? Is He without a peer? Is He unique? Is He indeed *the* way, *the* truth, and *the* life (John 14:6) or merely *a* way, *a* truth, and *a* life? We might consider the incomparable Christ and perhaps take a note from advertisers who advise us to compare and determine which is the best in everything from Cadillacs on down. Let us compare Jesus Christ and what He has given us to the founders of other religions and what has been given to their followers for three reasons: First, that we might see more clearly just who Jesus Christ is. As one philosopher has said, the only way that we really understand anything is by knowing what that thing is. I think we will know more clearly what Christ is when we look at the rest of the religions of the world.

Second, let us realize more appreciatively that which we have been given in Christ, if we are Christians. The fact that you are a member of a Christian church does not necessarily mean you are a Christian; but if you are truly a Christian, then I hope that you will see more clearly the tremendous privilege and blessing you have received.

Third, we need to better understand what our attitude toward the adherents of non-Christian religions should be. Should it be one of arrogance or hostility? Hardly! It should rather be one of pity and compassion and love. Most Americans do not realize the plight of pagans. They have visualized some sort of an imaginary person who really does not represent the great masses of the world that struggle in the dark morass of their paganism. The evolutionist would tell us that religions are evolved from a polytheistic animism all the way up to the monotheistic faith of the day, but the Bible tells us something different. Interestingly enough, archaeologists, in the last fifty years, have been uncovering one fact after another to show us that behind all the vastness of the polytheistic and animistic religions of the world is a basic core of original monotheism, which has been covered up. The Bible tells us that people originally knew God, but they became vain in their imaginations. Their foolish hearts were darkened, and supposing themselves to be wise, they became fools and worshiped and served the creature rather than the Creator who is blessed forever. So we find people everywhere worshiping snakes and creeping things and birds and all sorts of idols, so that the evolution of religion is in fact a devolution from the original revelation of God.

The first religion we might consider is one that is held by hundreds of millions of people around the world from Africa to the South Seas. It is known as *animism*. This is the religion of the aborigines of most of the continents of the world. It is the primitive people's religion, the most primitive religion on the face of the earth. Animism comes from the Latin word *anima*, which means mind or soul. It is based on the idea that inanimate objects are possessed of a living soul—a living spirit—something which lives within them. Now, they have at least come to discern between the material and the spiritual world. They have a very real consciousness of a spiritual world, and they also have a consciousness of a God who is a single, supreme Being. Every animistic religion of Africa has a word for God. But the people are not interested in God, because they believe that He has turned them over to some lesser deities after creating them. They are constantly involved in placating these lesser deities or spirits who are mostly hostile. They also believe that the spirits of people pass into something else—perhaps into a stone or a tree or a crocodile or a river or a bird. It is important to understand animism because it is a substratum that underlies and penetrates every pagan religion. It has elements that can be found in almost every one of them. Here you see the beginning of a concept of the transmigration of the soul or reincarnation that is held in a number of religions. Since these people live in a world that is controlled by savagery and oppression and that has no real moral law, savagery prevails. Animism is a way of darkness. These people live in constant dread and fear of this spiritual world that haunts them everywhere. You often see reverence, dread and awe, and worship of such things as snakes found among the animists. Fetishism, black magic, and voodooism are all a part of this horrible primitive religion of man. This is not something for which we would exchange the glories of Christ!

Now, let us go from that to the religions of the great continent of Asia, the subcontinent of Asia—India, and the Hindu religion. *Hindu* comes from the word *Hind* (from which we get India), and it is indeed the religion of India and was never meant to be evangelistic. To be a Hindu, one must be born one. In about 1500 B.C., at the time when the Israelites were suffering persecution in Egypt, the Aryans, a people from the Iranian plateau and related to the Persians, came into the north of India and conquered the aborigines who were called Dravidians and subjugated these dark-skinned people. This was the beginning of the most basic element of the Hindu religion—caste. Hinduism is the only religion in the world that has a caste system as part of it. Now the Sanskrit word for caste, *varna*, means color. It is a color system of segregation. There are the Brahmans, the highest caste; the Kshatriyas, who are the noblemen; the Vaisyas, who are the mercantile people; and finally the Sudras, who are the lowest caste individuals. These castes have nothing to do with each other. Furthermore, people in the lowest caste have no hope of salvation and cannot even read the sacred books of the Hindus because they are not allowed to come close to a Brahman. A Sudra may come no closer than sixty-four feet from a high caste Brahman lest the air he exhales should contaminate the Brahman.

This system developed from a rather simplistic polytheism, where some 330 million gods and goddesses were worshiped, to a more sophisticated philosophic pantheism. In the later writings, called the Upanishads, everything is God. There is, according to the teaching of Hinduism, the World

Soul, Brahman. This is God, and there is a part of this in every one of us. These people feel that the great thing to be understood is that only the World Soul or *atman* is real, and that part of it dwells within us. The rest of the world is an illusion. It does not exist. Our body does not exist. Pain does not exist. Death does not exist. The world does not exist. "All is Brahman and Brahman is all." Hindus hope through understanding that the world does not really exist and that all is God and by meditating upon the great existing God, they can finally, through a number of reincarnations, achieve *nirvana*. They feel that this may take thousands of reincarnations of continual suffering. Though the original religion of India was optimistic, as it progressed it became pessimistic, a change which always occurs where there is paganism and idolatry. Life becomes worse and worse until people come to the place where they hate life itself. The great thing they are looking for is the extinction of life, nirvana, where one finally becomes extinct and ceases to be reborn into further cycles of life, where the individual soul drops back into the ocean and ceases to have any individual consciousness.

About 560 B.C. a prince of the Sakyas, named Siddhartha Gautama, was born in Northern India. He was wealthy. His father was a prince, and he was kept within a palace and was shielded from all of the world until he was twenty-nine years old. He knew nothing about the suffering of the world. Finally he went out and saw a man who was sick, another who was dying, another who was crippled, and one who was dead. He was so shaken by this experience that he set about to find an answer to the cause of suffering. After six years of searching, he had not found the answer, so he finally determined to sit down under a Bo tree and not to get up until he found it. After many days, he finally received enlightenment and discovered the cause of suffering in the world. The Hindu had said the reason for suffering is ignorance. People think that the world is real and therefore they suffer, and we must change their thinking. "Not so," said Gautama, now known as the Buddha, The Enlightened One. (*Buddha* is related to the word *bode* or *forebode*, to know.) He said the reason is not in the mind or the intellect. The reason is in the emotions. Buddha was not really a religious founder; he was a psychologist and was concerned about people's emotions—basically about the matter of desire. He said the reason people suffer is that they desire things they cannot have, and if they would just cease to desire things, they would not suffer anymore.

Of course, while Hinduism and Buddhism were both looking for the answer to the problem of suffering, they were looking for the answer to the wrong problem. The problem is sin, which did not concern them but which causes suffering. All Buddha had to offer people was simply a quicker way to reach extinction, so that by simply one life, one could leap immediately into the ocean of extinction called nirvana. Buddhism is not a religion. Let me quote from a prestigious Buddhist magazine, *The Buddhist*, "It is etiologically incorrect to refer to Buddhism as a religion." A Buddhist does not admit the existence of God. Buddha was an atheist. He denied any God or gods. He denied prayer. He denied all the priests and the Brahmans. He was a psychologist, as Freud was, and not a religious leader. Buddhism is not a religion.

A man by the name of K'ung Fu-tzu, whom we know as Confucius, was born in China in the year 551 B.C. He was a wise man who taught many good things; but he, like Buddha, did not found a religion. He taught filial piety: the relation of subjects to emperors, husbands to wives, parents to children, and elders to youngsters. This is what Confucius taught. Toward God, he was an agnostic. When someone asked him, "What about life after death?" he said, "How can we know about death, when we do not even know about life?" This is the hope that Confucius offered—nothing!

Then, of course, there was Shintoism, wherein the emperors of Japan were worshiped. That was given the death blow in 1945. When you go to Africa, you have Islam. There Mohammed, six hundred years after Christ, gave to the people the Koran, which is a distortion of much of the Old Testament of the Bible. It offers a sensual paradise and is a belief that was spread with the sword. Whereas millions of Christians died because they were unwilling to renounce their Christian faith, the Moslems had a strange way of proselytizing. They took a sword, and if the person was not willing to become a Moslem, off went the head! They spread their religion throughout much of North Africa and Northern India, by conquest, in just that way.

Judaism is simply the biblical religion with its head cut off—truncated without Christ—the heart of which is a sacrificial system which says that without the shedding of blood there is no remission of sins. All of the sacrificial system was ended with the destruction of Jerusalem, so now Judaism has a vacuum at its core. There is nothing else that people can turn to except Christ.

How vastly different are all these religions from Jesus Christ! There is only one thing they really have in common. They all teach something about ethics or about God—not necessarily about both. Jesus is not just a teacher, as so many people superficially suppose today. That is not really why He came.

There are three great differences between Christ and the founders of all other religions. These differences are observed in the three great festivals we have in Christianity. The first is Christmas. Jesus Christ is an incarnate deity. He is God Himself having come into this world. Buddha never thought about this. There was no God anywhere to come to his world. Confucius would have abhorred the idea. Mohammed would have screamed blasphemy if anyone had suggested that he was God. None of these people made this claim, but Jesus Christ does. He claims to be God Almighty before whom every knee shall bow. His deity is confirmed by a life that is absolutely unique. His life is unlike any other life that has ever existed, for it was the only sinless life the world has ever known.

Dr. Saunders presents some aspects of the uniqueness of Jesus Christ. I think they are interesting. Let me share them with you. One way in which the life of Jesus Christ was different from anyone that ever existed before or since is that Christ never withdrew or modified any statement He ever made. I wonder how many of you could say the same. How many times I have had to correct my opinion as time has gone on. Jesus never did—not once.

Another thing that we notice about Him is that He lacked a trait we often say is the trait of a great man—the ability, the strength to apologize. When two people have been at odds with each other, I have always said, "You know, I can tell which of you is the larger person—he is the one who apologizes." But Jesus never once apologized for anything He ever did or said. It was not because people never got mad at Him. No matter what the circumstances were, He never apologized. Why? He was never wrong. He, unlike ourselves, was never wrong about anything!

Another amazing fact is that He never sought advice from anyone. Though He was born in obscurity, He never sought advice. Unlike Confucius, He was not well educated. He was not educated at all. This Man never learned. He was never taught. Unlike Buddha, He was never enlightened. He always knew. Unlike Mohammed, who could neither read nor write, He was never ignorant. He knew everything. He never sought the advice of any soul, though He came to bring a plan to change the world. He went among the doctors and taught them; He corrected the scribes and the Pharisees. Moses sought seventy advisors; and Solomon, the wisest man that ever lived, sought the advice of others; but Jesus never did. He never went to the first grade, but He never asked anyone anything. Why? Because He knew everything—because He is God.

Another amazing thing is that He never once troubled to justify His ambiguous behavior. When He was asleep in the back of the boat and the storm came and the disciples were rowing and bailing, what was Jesus doing? He was sleeping in the back of the boat! When they roused Him and asked, "Master, carest thou not if we perish?" (Mark 4:38) did He help bail the water out of the boat? No! He said to the sea, "Peace, be still" (Mark 4:39). When Jesus received word that Lazarus had died, He stayed right where He was for four days. Then, when He arrived, Martha said, "Lord, if thou hadst been here, my brother had not died" (John 11:21). Did Jesus apologize? No, not a word! He just allowed time and the unfolding of God's plan to justify all that He did.

Another amazing facet of the personality of Jesus is that He never asked for prayer for Himself. How many times have I asked people to pray for me. Jesus never asked anyone to pray for Him. Never! He never even permitted it. What about the three that went into the Garden of Gethsemane? He said, "Come and watch with me." He said, "Pray for *yourselves*, lest ye enter into temptation." He never asked anyone to pray for Him (Mark 14:32–38). We do not need to pray for God. He never allowed anyone to, and this is amazing, because here He was, the lowliest of men, the most humble of men that ever lived; and yet He allowed people to fall on their faces before Him and to worship Him. When John did this before an angel, the angel said, "Stand up on thy feet" (see Rev. 22:8). But Jesus never did.

What were Jesus' strong points? He did not have any— not a one! To have a strong point, you must have a weak point, and Jesus did not have any weak points. Other men are noted for some one faculty or talent: Moses was the meekest of all men, Job was the patient one. But Jesus was altogether lovely in every way—the incomparable symmetry of the perfections of Jesus Christ. What a balance He had! It has been said that we try so hard to walk that balanced line, and we fail so continuously. We try to be spiritual, and we end up aesthetic; we try to be liberal in our views of this world and its pleasures, and we end up buried under the world; we try to be scrupulous in our conduct, and we end up as legalists; we try to follow the high and noble aspirations of liberty, and we end up in licentiousness; we try to be fervent, and we end up fanatical; we try to be gentle, and we waver and fail to follow the truth. But Jesus mixed truth with gentleness in a perfect mixture. He never once rectified or adjusted His personality, because Jesus is God.

The second great difference between Jesus and the founders of others religions is observed on Good Friday. Jesus came to do something that the founder of no other religion ever did. He came to die—not simply to teach—He came to die for our sins. This Confucius did not do. When he was eighty years old, disillusioned by the fact that people would not follow his teachings, Confucius said, "The mountains crumble and the great beam is broken and the flower falls to the ground," and he lay down and died. Buddha died of food poisoning, but Jesus gave His life for the world. What a difference!

Someone has illustrated this difference with the story of a man in a pit—a deep, vile, filthy pit with a huge serpent in there with him that he is trying to avoid. He has fallen into this ghastly pit! What happens? Well, along comes an animist, and he looks down into the pit and sees the serpent. His eyes open wide, and he flees into the jungle lest the same evil spirit should heave him into the pit. Then along comes the Confucianist and he says, "Ah, a great man never falls in a pit, but walks circumspectly. Henceforth you will look where you walk." The Hindu comes along and says, "Ah, my brother, you think that you are in a great black pit, but that is the error of mortal mind. The fact is that all is Brahman and Brahman is all, and this external world is merely illusion. The pit does not exist. Think, 'There is no pit, there is no pit, there is no serpent,' and all will be well. Peace." Then comes the Moslem, who sees the man down in the pit and says, "I will help you, my friend." And he reaches down and grabs him by the arm and pulls him halfway out of the pit and draws his knife and says, "However, you will become a Moslem, won't you?" The man responds, "I can never do that!" So back he goes into the pit. Then comes the Buddhist, who looks down and says, "Dear friend, you are suffering greatly in that pit, and the reason you are suffering is because you want to get out of the pit. It is your desire that is making you miserable. What you must come to is a cessation of all desire. Then you won't mind being in the pit." And then Jesus comes and looks with compassionate eyes at the man in the pit. And into that foul and filthy pit He leaps between the man and the serpent, who rears his ugly head and strikes at the Savior and sinks his fangs into His side. As the venom of that serpent flows into the blood of Jesus, He lifts the man out of the pit. That, my friends, is a Savior. That is the difference between Christianity and all the other religions.

The third great difference is celebrated at Easter. Confucius died and was buried. Lao-tse wandered off and died with his buffalo. Buddha rotted with food poisoning. Jesus rose from the dead and by His resurrection from the dead He demonstrated that He is indeed the Son of God with power. By His life, death, and resurrection He declares that He is God Himself.

Napoleon, in his last days, turned to the Scriptures to find the meaning of life, which he had not found in all of his fame, and discovered who Jesus was. He said to General Bertrand, who was an atheist, "I know men; and I tell you that Jesus Christ is not a man. Superficial minds see a resemblance between Christ and the founders of empires and the gods of other religions. That resemblance does not exist. We can say to the authors of every other religion, 'You are neither gods, nor the agents of the Deity.' What do these gods, so boastful, know more than other mortals; these legislators, Greek or Roman; this Numa; this Lycurgus; these priests of India or of Memphis; this Confucius; this Mohammed?—absolutely nothing. They have made a perfect chaos of mortals. There is not one among them all who has said anything new in reference to our future destiny, to the soul, to the essence of

God, to the creation. Enter the sanctuaries of paganism: you there find perfect chaos, a thousand contradictions, war between the gods, the immobility of sculpture, the division and the rending of unity, the parceling out of the divine attributes mutilated or denied in their essence. It is not so with Christ. Everything in Him astonishes me. His spirit overawes me, and His will confounds me. Between him and whoever else in the world, there is no possible term of comparison. He is truly a Being by Himself. Bertrand, if you do not perceive that Jesus Christ is God, very well: then I did wrong to make you a general."

Jesus rose from the dead by the power of the Father, who has given Him a name which is above every other name. At the name of Jesus every knee shall bow (see Phil. 2:9–10). Is He the Lord of your life? Is He the Savior of your life? Friend, have you been so busy with your headlong rush through this hedonism of materialistic America that you have failed even to look around and to consider? Some of you are so blind that you do not even know you are in the pit!

O God, grant us a compassion and pity on those that live in darkness and fear without hope in this life and in the life to come. We pray that Thou wilt grant us a new zeal to take the love of Jesus Christ and that hope of everlasting bliss which He alone can give to all of the world. And now we pray for any who have never met Him. May they come to know Him personally as they invite Him into their hearts and lives, for we ask it in that blessed name which is above every name, even Jesus Christ the Lord. *Amen.*

Repentance

I tell you, Nay: but, except ye repent, ye shall all likewise perish.

Luke 13:3

I tell you, Nay: but, except ye repent, ye shall all likewise perish." These are the words of Jesus Christ concerning repentance. In a way, it's a strange doctrine because repentance itself will not save you. Yet you cannot be saved without it! Merely repenting of one's sin does not guarantee an entrance into heaven. Humanists say all a person must do to enter the kingdom of heaven is feel a true contrition for sins, confess, and repent of them, and endeavor to lead a good life. This is repentance, but not the kind that will gain the forgiveness of our sins or admission into eternal life. Why? Because a person must give Jesus Christ a proper place in his or her life. You see, God's law has been broken, and the transgression of the law demands a penalty must be paid. A change of heart will not suffice.

While many churches ignore this doctrine, the Bible gives it considerable emphasis. Both Old and New Testaments call upon people to repent. Noah was a preacher of righteousness, calling people to leave their wicked ways and turn to God. All the prophets were preachers of repentance. In fact, the name *Nahum* comes from a root meaning "repentance." Both the major and minor prophets called people to repent. John the Baptist said, "Who hath warned you to flee from the wrath to come? Bring forth therefore fruits meet for repentance" (Matt. 3:7–8).

When Christ reached His thirtieth year (the time for the priest to begin his priestly function), our Great High Priest was baptized and began His work as prophet and priest. How did Jesus begin His ministry? Matthew says, "From that time Jesus began to preach, and to say, Repent" (Matt. 4:17). The burden of His heart and ministry for this world of sinners was, Repent! "Except ye repent, ye shall all likewise perish" (Luke 13:3). Many of His parables, such as the prodigal son, deal with the subject of repentance. After Jesus' resurrection, on the road to Emmaus, He said to the two: "Thus it is written, and thus it behoved Christ to suffer, and to rise from the dead the third day: and that repentance and remission of sins should be preached in his name among all nations, beginning at Jerusalem" (Luke 24:46–47). Christ began, continued, and ended His ministry with the same word—repent!

At Pentecost, when the Spirit of God was poured out and the church began its distinctively Christian ministry, Peter preached the first sermon. After the people were reminded what God had done, they said, "What must we do?" And Peter said, "Repent!"(see Acts 2:38).

Paul said he was called by God to preach that people should exercise repentance toward God and faith in the Lord Jesus Christ. "And the times of this ignorance God winked at; but now commandeth all men every where to repent" (Acts 17:30). The letters to the churches in the Book of Revelation abound in commands to repent. Eight times in these letters Jesus walks among His churches, symbolic of the churches of all times, and says, "Repent . . . or else I will come unto thee quickly, and will remove thy candlestick out of his place" (Rev. 2:5). Fifty-three times in the New Testament people are called to repent or told they must have repentance.

There are many who delude themselves with the false hope of being in favor with God because of something they may have done. The Westminster Confession says that such hope will perish with them. Jesus Christ said, "Except ye repent, ye shall all likewise perish" (Luke 13:3). If this is such an essential doctrine, why is it not heralded more clearly from our pulpits today? R. B. Kuiper says that it is because people have lost sight of two things: first, the real meaning of sin. They see sin as a trifle, a peccadillo, something they excuse as being part of their human nature. They forget their nature is fallen, debased, depraved, and that man is nothing like God first made him. They do not see that sin inevitably brings forth death. And secondly, people have lost their vision of the holy God. They do not lift up their eyes, because if they once saw God, they would abhor themselves and repent in dust and ashes.

Repentance and faith are inseparable in Scripture. There can be no genuine repentance without faith. And there is no genuine faith without repentance. The two go together as heads and tails on one coin. You may have a false faith which is merely an intellectual assent and which brings forth no true repentance or amendment of your lifestyle, or a repentance without saving faith which causes you to rely upon your own strivings. This becomes a bootstrap repentance where the person endeavors to do better, but trusts in his own works.

Because the human soul is made up of mind, heart, and will, all three must become involved in true faith and repentance. We must intellectually grasp that sin, because of its heinousness, will inevitably be punished by God. We must also intellectually grasp and understand the divine remedy for sin. We must come to know the way of salvation as it has been divinely appointed by God and must not be deluded by some false plan of salvation of our own making. We must understand that it is only through Christ's grace and death on the cross that we have eternal hope. But even understanding will not be sufficient. It must go beyond the mind to the heart, to the affection. We must come to God with a contrite heart: "A broken and contrite heart, O God, thou wilt not despise" (Ps. 51:17).

People may be moved to tears by a sermon and even decide they're going to do something about their sin. But if their decision is not based on a proper understanding of the gospel, they will trust in their own efforts to do better and soon be back wallowing in the mud of sin, despair, and frustration.

There are some who have been reared in the church and suppose themselves to be Christians but have never by an act of their will renounced their sins and turned to Jesus Christ. But nothing less will suffice for repentance! It is only as we see the awfulness of our own sins and truly desire in our hearts to turn from them and embrace the Savior, that God accepts our repentance. This repentance is not something we can do of ourselves; it is not merely an effort to turn over a new leaf and try to do better. Second Timothy 2:24–25 says, "And the servant of the Lord must not strive; but be gentle . . . instructing those that oppose themselves; if God peradventure will give them repentance." They glorified God because He granted unto the Gentiles repentance. Repentance, then, is a gift of God's grace that transforms the heart, mind, and will.

I once heard Jerome Hines sing a memorable part from the *Messiah*, "Who shall stand when He appeareth?" My question is, Will you stand in that day? You will not unless you have both repented of your sins and turned to trust in the cross of Christ. You will not unless you have seen your righteousness as nothing but filthy rags; unless you have seen all your good deeds as tainted with self, vanity, and pride. You will not unless you have trusted only in the righteousness of Christ and His atoning blood.

Have you repented of your sins, or are you deluded into believing that you can live in sin and then live in heaven? The

Word of God to you is unmistakable. In that great day they shall come forth from the graves—the rich and poor, wise and foolish, righteous and unrighteous, wicked and saints, rulers and slaves, great men and small (see Rev. 20:12–15). From the depth of the sea, the ships shall give up their dead; those that have lain long in cemeteries shall come forth. When Christ shall speak, they shall hear His voice and all come forth—willing and unwilling. They shall arise. They shall stand before God. And they shall be judged. Only if our names are written in the Lamb's Book of Life will we enter into eternal life. Will your name be written there?

Jesus Christ says, "Except ye repent, ye shall all likewise perish" (Luke 13:3).

> O God, deliver us from being deceived. Grant unto us a new sense of the heinousness of our sins and the holiness of God. May we turn from them all to walk in the ways of new obedience. Cause us to mourn for our sins and turn unto Thee, O Lord Jesus Christ, who has been lifted up on a cross that we might be saved if we will repent and believe. *Amen.*

7

Faith

For by grace are ye saved through faith; and that not of your-selves: it is the gift of God: not of works, lest any man should boast.

Ephesians 2:8–9

The occasion was a typical Sunday church service, but the locale was behind the iron curtain in Communist Eastern Europe. The service was progressing as usual when suddenly two Communist soldiers brandishing submachine guns kicked open the door. With flailing arms and angry voices, they denounced the Christians and their vile worship. "Such worms as you have no right to exist upon the face of the earth!" they shouted. "We are going to shoot all of you! However, those who are willing to denounce their faith and deny Christ can move immediately to the right side of the sanctuary, and you will be free to leave." A portion of the congregation got up and moved. The soldiers then commanded them to get out. Most of the congregation sat motionless in their pews. When the doors were closed, the Communists turned to those sitting before them. "We, too, are

Christians," they said. "We've come to fellowship with you, but we first had to get rid of the hypocrites."

I like this story because it perfectly illustrates this important matter of faith. Faith is important because it is the key that opens the door to the Christian life and all Christ has done for us. It's the key that opens the door to heaven. The Scripture says, "He that believeth . . . shall be saved; but he that believeth not shall be damned" (Mark 16:16).

I would like to consider this matter in three aspects: first, the nature of faith; second, the object of faith; third, the origin of faith. Many people bring themselves to church to hear words they have not the slightest intention of obeying. This is exceedingly strange when we consider the secular world where belief and faith are easily understood.

If, for instance, a person is told his business venture is entirely spurious and is presented with the facts as to why this is so, he will listen to the reasons and then decide to accept or reject them. If he believes, he will immediately remove all property from the misrepresented venture. If someone comes to you and says in desperate tones, "The rear of your house is on fire!" and you believe him, you will immediately leap from your chair, call the fire department, and flee from the premises with your family.

If a man is shown an X ray that contains a dark and ominous spot representing sure death unless he takes immediate steps for its removal, and if he believes the diagnosis, he will immediately place himself in the surgeon's hands. There is no question about it!

In the secular world, belief is plain, simple, and understood by all; but when we come to Christian truth, things seem to change. Most hear over and over again that "the wages of sin is death," that "God is angry with the wicked every day," that "he that believeth not shall be damned," that God "will by no means clear the guilty," that "Except ye repent, ye shall likewise perish" (Rom. 6:23; Ps. 7:11; Mark 16:16; Exod. 34:7; Luke 13:3). Those who are ashamed of Christ in this world will find that He is ashamed of them in the world to come. They hear also that God offers forgiveness, a gracious salvation, and eternal life, and that this offer will not continue indefinitely. They hear that a time is coming when the day of grace will irretrievably be gone and the opportunity lost. They know that for them this moment is completely uncertain. They know that in a moment they have not considered, there may be a sudden pain in the chest or a screeching of brakes and crashing of glass, and death will transport them into eternal woe.

This they hear, but though God calls loudly and clearly to change from one path of life and to enter upon another, they neglect to do anything about it. By a calculation of chances, on which they would not risk so much as a penny in the mercantile world, they deceive and assure themselves that they are able to face such a risk. Though they hear these words often, many do not practice the truths they have heard. Professing to believe, they act throughout the week in point-blank opposition to what they have heard on Sunday. Such is the condition of multitudes of people who call themselves Christians.

Now the question I propose is this: Does such indolent assent deserve the name of faith? Do these people in fact believe? Place this question before any secular jury and the verdict would be inevitable. When people in the secular world believe in a business deal, they act on it. Regardless of what you might have thought about the people who fled that morning from the church in Eastern Europe, there is one unmistakable thing—they believed the soldiers! The man who tells you he believes what you've told him about his business picture and does nothing about it only invites you to doubt his word. The person who says, "Oh, the house is on fire? Yes, of course—" and then goes back to reading the sports page is telling you he doesn't believe you. The man who leaves the doctor's office and does nothing as a result of the declaration of the physician is simply declaring to the world that he does not believe the diagnosis. The secular world is not befuddled; it knows what *believe* means. It knows that if a person believes something concerning a matter which involves action, he will inevitably do that which his belief demands.

The principle is exactly the same in religious matters. People who do not act upon what they have heard are simply people who do not believe. People who are not moved to a correspondent action or volition by what they hear are people without faith. Martin Luther said that many people suppose themselves to have faith, but they don't know what it is. True faith is a divine work of God in our hearts that makes us new in all our faculties. It is a busy, active thing which doesn't stop to ask if good works should be done. To put it in the words of our Confession of Faith, "We are justified by faith alone." It is faith alone that is the instrument of justification. The faith that alone justifies is never alone in the justified individual. It is always accompanied by those graces that will inevitably be produced by a living faith. James said, "Faith without works is dead" (James 2:26), which simply means that a faith that does not produce a transformed life is a vain, empty illusion and is no real faith at all.

There have been many long dissertations on the matter of faith—most of which confuse more than clarify. Innumerable theologians have given themselves sedulously to distinguishing the various types of faith, the various organs of believing, the various types of mental assent, et cetera. Average laypeople who read such works come to the conclusion that faith is something that is reserved for the mystical saint or the obtuse theologian. Though the Bible says that if they believe, they will have eternal life (John 6:47), they find themselves incapable of understanding what is meant by belief. The faith that justifies is not something different in nature from that which we know as faith and believing.

How did Christ begin His ministry? Did He begin by establishing a school where He spent the first year or so in long theological and philosophical arguments about the nature of this new thing called faith that He was going to reveal to the world? And after many dissertations and explanations about the meaning of faith, did He say to the people, "Now that you know what *believe* means, you can believe"? He did no such thing! Rather, we read in Scripture that Jesus began to preach and to say, "Repent and believe" (Mark 1:15). Throughout Scripture there is every indication that Jesus used the words *believe* and *faith* in a way that all would understand. There was nothing confusing about it. Thus, to have faith is to believe; to believe is to have faith.

When I come to see that something is true (not merely understanding it, but seeing that it is true), then I have faith in it—whether I like it or not. I may accept it willingly, or I may accept it unwillingly. But if I believe it to be true, then indeed I have faith in it. This is the meaning of faith.

Perhaps you think you do believe, but you don't have the temperament or disposition to serve Christ, to give yourself unstintingly for Him, to bear witness to His gospel as He commands, to read His Scripture, to pray, to fulfill His Great Commission, and indeed endeavor by all you have within you to walk in the ways of complete and new obedience. No, it's not that there is something different about your disposition. What I would have you see is that you do not believe. Coiled deep down in your soul is the lurking serpent of unbelief. If you believed, you would be transformed by that belief. "If any man be in Christ, he is a new creature [a new creation]" (2 Cor. 5:17). This is the nature of belief; there is nothing confusing about it. Do you believe the Word of God? Our Confession of Faith states clearly that by this faith a Christian believeth to be true whatsoever is revealed in the Word, for the authority of God Himself is speaking therein. There it is. He believes it to be true. When you truly believe something to be true, you will invariably act according to it. Therefore the problems with our behavior are simply evidences of our unbelief.

What are we to believe? What is the object of our faith? In the broadest sense, it is the whole Word of God, whatever is revealed in His Word. And we act differently upon each particular passage—yielding obedience to the commands and embracing the promises of God for this life and that which is to come. It is believing the Word of God. This is faith. But this is a faith that inevitably works by love. The supreme object of our faith is the person of Jesus Christ Himself. As our Confession continues, the principal acts of saving faith are accepting, receiving, and resting upon Christ alone for justification, sanctification, and eternal life. This is the principal act of saving faith: receiving Him, resting upon Christ who comes to us in all His grace and glory as our High Priest, our Sacrifice, our Surety, who offers Himself in our stead, and who promises us eternal life. Our acceptance of Him is based upon the promises of God's Word. Scripture says, "Whosoever believeth in him should not perish, but have everlasting life" (John 3:16); "Him that cometh to me I will in no wise cast out" (John 6:37); "He that believeth on [me] is not condemned" (John 3:18). Faith is believing what God has said to be true.

Many of those who do not have faith are those who believe some false or distorted notion that does not allow them to understand or believe what God's Word says. They suppose the Bible presents Christ as a taskmaster requiring them to do something to save themselves. They do not understand that Jesus Christ is not a taskmaster but indeed our Surety who fulfilled God's demands and died for our sins. When we come to believe His Word and trust in Him, we are reconciled to God, our sins are forgiven, and we are made heirs of eternal life, adopted into His family, and become the children of God. When we believe that we are saved, our lives are invariably transformed.

But why the problem of unbelief? The problem is we are blind and cannot see Him because Satan has deluded our minds. Jesus said, "Having eyes ye see not" (Mark 8:18). Blind!

Groping in darkness! Christ said, "Except a man be born again, he cannot see the kingdom of God" (John 3:3)—much less enter into it!

After talking to a lovely young lady about the meaning of Christ, I said, "If you really want Him to come into your heart, go home and ask Him to come in, to open your eyes, and to give you eternal life." She called several days later to tell me she had received Christ. "And," she said, "for the first time in my life the worship service means something to me. It's a whole new world!"

"Except a man be born again, he cannot see the kingdom of God" (John 3:3). Faith comes by the Spirit of God at work in our hearts, and yet many cannot believe because their hearts are hardened in sin. But I say to you, look unto Him who has died in your place and paid your penalty. Look unto Him whose hands are extended unto you and offering you life eternal. There is life for a look at the Crucified One. Look—and believe!

Father, we pray that Your Spirit may graciously and sovereignly open the eyes of the blind that they may see the light of Your glory shining in the face of Jesus Christ. May they take hold of Him by faith and be transformed by His love. In His lovely name. *Amen.*

Justification

Therefore we conclude that a man is justified by faith without the deeds of the law.

Romans 3:28

In this chapter we come to the pinnacle of the *ordo salutis*—the way of salvation. We come to holy ground. We come to the great central theme of the doctrines of redemption in the church of Christ. We come to justification. This is the doctrine that broke the shackles from the soul of Martin Luther and set him free, exalting in his God and glorying in the mercy of Jesus Christ. This is the doctrine that he took upon his tongue and with flaming eloquence proclaimed all over Europe. This is the doctrine that became the very heartbeat of the Protestant Reformation. This is the doctrine without which there would be no Protestantism. John Calvin said, "This is the foremost pillar of religion." The great Geerhardus Vos said, "It is the pivotal point around which all else turns." The immortal Bavinck said, "This is the article of the creed by which the Church either stands or falls."

The doctrine of justification *is* the gospel of our Lord Jesus Christ. Here the full-orbed mercy and grace of God comes into its own. But, alas, we live in a time almost like that of Luther's. The darkness of spiritual ignorance has so pervaded the minds of people that vast numbers in this so-called Christian America live in abject ignorance of this central teaching of the Christian faith, this central doctrine of the Bible. I think it can be safely said that without at least a rudimentary knowledge of the basic principle involved in this doctrine, no person will ever see heaven. Truly by this the church stands or falls, and our souls stand or fall with it. If this be the case, then indeed most of the church is sadly fallen in our day. And how great is that fall! From that time only 450 years ago when this was the clarion call, the trumpet blast, that woke countless hundreds of thousands from their death in sin unto life eternal, we have come to our time when in myriads of churches across our land the question What is justification? would meet merely with a raised eyebrow and a questioning look. "The just shall live by faith" was the watchword of the Protestant Reformation.

Let us now consider the nature of this doctrine and its importance to us. In this doctrine lies the truth that answers the greatest need of humanity, How can man be rightly related to God? In the Book of Job, probably the oldest book of the Bible, Job cries out from the depths of his heart, asking how a sinful man can ever stand in the presence of a Holy God. This is the cry that has been wrung from the blanched lips of countless millions of penitent sinners down through the centuries. But it is a cry that is strangely unheard in our day. Why? Well, the reason is not hard to come by. I think it is simply that man is so abysmally far from God for the most part that he is even ignorant of the fact that he is separated from God. He has no concept whatsoever of sin. He has no feeling of remorse for it. He has no awareness of the righteousness and holiness of God and, consequently, no feeling of any need for justification. He can quite adequately justify

himself in his own eyes. If sin is considered at all, it is merely
a peccadillo of some sort to be easily rationalized away, or at
most adjusted by a visit to the psychiatrist.

John Murray, the famous theologian, has presented our
predicament tersely in these words:

> How can man be right with God? The answer, of course, is that
> we cannot be right with Him for we are all wrong with Him.
> And we are all wrong with Him because we have all sinned and
> come short of the glory of God. Far too frequently we fail to
> entertain the gravity of this fact; hence the reality of our sin and
> the reality of the wrath of God upon us for our sin do not come
> into our reckoning at all. This is the reason why the grand arti-
> cle of justification does not ring the bells in the innermost depths
> of our souls today. And this is the reason why the gospel of jus-
> tification is to such an extent a meaningless sound in the world
> of the church of the twentieth century. We are not imbued with
> the profound sense of the reality of God; of His majesty and His
> holiness. And sin, if reckoned with at all, is little more than a
> misfortune or a maladjustment. If we are to appreciate that which
> is central in the gospel, if the jubilee trumpet is to find its echo
> again in our hearts, our thinking must be revolutionized by the
> realism of the wrath of God, of the reality and gravity of our
> guilt, and of the divine condemnation upon it.

Those are words that are seldom heard in our day when
sin is glossed over, ignored, or snickered at—but God is not
impressed with our light attitude toward that which He hates.
God has sworn that He will "visit [our] transgression with
the rod, and [our] iniquity with stripes" (Ps. 89:32). There is
a divine penalty for sin. Twentieth-century man has endeavored to forget it, to deny it, to ignore it, to turn his back upon
it, to get away from it, to escape from it, and to hope in some
way that it will just go away and leave him alone. But it will
not! The reality of man's guilt has filled to overflowing the
mental institutions of this nation until they sprawl as endless
cities. Wing after wing of these institutions is filled with peo-

ple who are there primarily because their lives are overwhelmed and crushed by their guilt which they've striven to
ignore and to deny.

When will we face reality for the way it is and seek God's
remedy for it instead of daubing at the surface blemishes of
the fatal cancer within? Even Freud, unbeliever that he was,
in his psychoanalytic studies probed deep into the soul of
humanity. There, as he plunged down into the subbasement
of the human soul, which he called the id, he found lurking
in all of the crevices and corners of that soul such foulness,
such unbelievable hate, such attitudes towards those whom
they were supposed to love, such lust and greed and pride,
that he himself was shocked at what he discovered. But he
was unknowingly putting his imprimatur on the Word of
God, which says, "For all have sinned, and come short of the
glory of God" (Rom. 3:23). "The heart is deceitful . . . and
desperately wicked: who can know it? I the Lord search the
heart . . ." (Jer. 17:9–10).

It is not until the apostle Paul has impressed upon us this
fact of our guilt that he even begins to bring up the subject
of justification. In the first chapter of the Book of Romans,
his theme is that all the Gentiles have sinned and God has
given them up to condemnation. In the second chapter his
theme is that all of the Jews have sinned and God has given
them up to condemnation. In the third chapter his theme is
that all, both Jews and Gentiles, are under sin; there is no difference—"For all have sinned, and come short of the glory
of God" (Rom. 3:23). "Therefore by the deeds of the law
there shall no flesh be justified in his sight" (Rom. 3:20). It is
only at that point, when every man and woman on the face
of this planet is shut up under sin, that Paul brings in the new
revelation of the mercy of God: "But now the righteousness
of God . . . is manifested" (Rom. 3:21). It is a free righteousness coming from God: "Being justified freely by his grace . . ."
(Rom. 3:24).

What then is the nature of this justification? The Westminster Catechism describes it most beautifully and aptly when it says that "justification is an act of God's free grace wherein He pardoneth all our sins and accepteth our persons as righteous—not for anything done by us or wrought in us, but only for the righteousness of Jesus Christ imputed to us and received by faith alone." Let us see what that means. First of all, we see that it is an act of God. It is God that justifies. Who is he who condemns? Man is constantly trying to justify himself. Someone said to me one time, "I can justify everything I've ever done to God." And though few people would be so rash as to make such a statement, this is exactly what most people are trying to do. I hear it constantly. They're trying to justify themselves; they're trying to plead innocent. "I'm not really so bad. I've really done some good. I've done this, but I haven't done those most wicked things." They're trying to justify themselves.

The doctrine of justification condemns every effort on the part of man to justify himself. It is God that justifies—not man. It is an act—not a process. It is done in the twinkling of the eye. In an instant, it is complete and perfect forever. It is an act of God's own grace. We see that it flows from the graciousness of Almighty God. It is not because of anything that we have done. We are not justified for our works, we are not justified because of our character, we are not justified because of our virtue or our goodness, of which the natural man in his unregenerate state has not one whit. We are justified purely by the grace and unmerited favor of God.

It is not anything done by us or wrought in us. Justification does not change our hearts, our souls, our lives one whit. It is something that is external to us. It is something that is declared *about* us by God. It is not God acting as a doctor or a surgeon in which He comes in and changes our hearts. Indeed God does internally change us, but that is regeneration and sanctification. Justification—that act whereby we begin the Christian life—is something that is outside of us altogether. It is a declaration about us; the declarative act of a judge about a sinner. In this declaration, God declares us to be righteous.

Some people have difficulty here. First of all, they do not understand what the word *justify* means. Let me say that it does not mean to make holy; it does not mean to make virtuous; it does not mean that it makes you good. You are no better the moment after you are justified than you were the moment before. You are not one bit holier the moment you are justified than you were before. We cannot separate justification and sanctification. God has placed His Spirit within us, and He is going to continue to work to sanctify us. But our justification is not something that comes at the end of this process when we have reached a certain level of acceptableness. We are justified as ungodly sinners. God justifies the ungodly. How could He do this? Justify does not mean to make holy.

But God justifies the ungodly. That this is true is evidently supported by the scriptural use of the words *to justify*. It is everywhere used as the opposite and antithesis of the words *to condemn*. The Bible says that the just judges are to justify the righteous and condemn the wicked. The Bible says it is an abomination in the sight of God if a judge justifies the wicked and condemns the righteous. It is a declaration about a person—not a change of his internal nature.

For example, "All the people . . . and the publicans, justified God," the Bible says. It would be absurd to suppose that a sinful publican could make God holy. They merely declared what He was. The Bible says that it is a sin to declare someone that is wicked to be righteous. But that's exactly what God does. And yet He does it without sin. How is it that He can do it? He does it in that wonderful way that is the gospel. He does it through His Son the Lord Jesus Christ. We are justified freely by His grace through the redemption that is in Christ Jesus, whom God set forth as a propitiation—a sacrifice—for our sins in order that He might be both the just and the justifier of those that believe in Jesus. It is through Christ that God does this.

The work of Christ may be divided into two parts. Theologians describe these as the *active* and the *passive* obedience of Christ. First of all, there are the thirty-three years in which He lived a perfect life, obeying every command of God. What kind of life does God require of you if you would ever enter heaven? He requires a perfect life. Do you have it? "Be ye therefore perfect, even as your Father which is in heaven is perfect" (Matt. 5:48). No, you don't have it. But Christ lived it for you—perfectly in your stead—and that life He is willing to give to you. The passive obedience of Christ (from which we get the word *passion*) is that which Christ endured for us, that which He suffered for us, primarily upon the cross. It is on the cross that Christ takes away all our sin, all our debt. But it is by His life, His active obedience, that we are given a perfect righteousness whereby we can stand in the presence of God.

If, as some suppose, justification were to be identified merely with forgiveness of sins, then we would merely be forgiven and brought to the place that Adam started. We would still have to work out our own righteousness, which Adam with his perfect nature was unable to do. (How much less would we be able to do it!) Therefore, in the act of justification God does two things. He first constitutes us righteous by imputing to our account the perfect righteousness of Jesus Christ. Having done this, He thereby declares what the situation now is. He thereby declares that the demands of the law have been met in our case, as Christ has fulfilled all of the obligations that we have to the law of God. He first constitutes us righteous and then declares us so to be; but it is with the righteousness of His Son. It might be somewhat analogous to graciously giving a man a large sum of money and then declaring him to be wealthy. This is what God does. He grants unto us the perfect righteousness of His Son and then declares us to be righteous. The Bible says that through the

disobedience of one man, many were accounted or constituted as sinners: so also through the obedience of One many
were constituted righteous through the righteousness of Jesus
Christ (see Rom. 5:19).

The doctrine of justification is infinitely more than mere
forgiveness. A governor or executive may forgive a criminal,
a judge may pardon one, and yet no judge has ever yet constituted a pardoned criminal righteous. Nor has he ever
adopted him into his family, nor has he ever given him an
inheritance, nor has he ever given him his name. But all of
these things and many others God has done for us. He
declares us to be righteous only through the righteousness of
Jesus Christ our Lord.

We must all someday stand before God. With what righteousness will you approach that awful throne? In that great
day when the heavens shall melt with fervent heat and the
earth shall be burnt up and all of the elements, how will you
approach unto the throne of God? Isaiah the prophet
describes it for us in this way: "I will greatly rejoice in the
LORD, my soul shall be joyful in my God; for he hath clothed
me with the garments of salvation, he hath covered me with
the robe of righteousness, as a bridegroom decketh himself
with ornaments, and as a bride adorneth herself with her jew-
els" (Isa. 61:10). As the hymn says,

> Jesus, Thy blood and righteousness,
> My beauty are, my glorious dress;
> Midst flaming worlds, in these arrayed,
> With joy shall I lift up my head.

This is the nature of justification. How do we receive it?
We receive it by faith, simply trusting in Christ. "Nothing in
my hand I bring, simply to thy cross I cling." But there's a
problem here for many. You see, this is such a humbling thing.
It requires that we, like the apostle Paul, look at all of those
so-called good works we have done that once were our pride

and joy and now count as dung that we may be found in Christ. We have not our own righteousness, which comes from trying to keep the law and in which we fail miserably every day; but we have the righteousness of God, which is by faith in Jesus Christ. It's a humbling thing. We have to admit our spiritual and moral bankruptcy, and this is what goes against the grain of the proud man and smites him right in the forehead.

The brilliant Dr. Gerstner has described the plight of the proud man in this way:

> Christ has done everything necessary for his salvation. Nothing now stands between the sinner and God but the sinner's "good works." Nothing can keep him from Christ but his delusion that he does not need Him—that he has good works of his own that can satisfy God. If men will only be convinced that they have no righteousness that is not as filthy rags; if men will see that there is none that doeth good, no, not one; if men will see that all are shut up under sin—then there will be nothing to prevent their everlasting salvation. All they need is need. All they must have is nothing. All that is required is acknowledged guilt. But, alas, sinners cannot part with their "virtues." They have none that are not imaginary, but they are real to them. So grace becomes unreal. The real grace of God they spurn in order to hold on to the illusory virtues of their own. Their eyes fixed on a mirage, they will not drink real water. They die of thirst in the midst of an ocean of Grace.

So, my friend, to what do you cling? Is it the illusory mirage of your own righteousness? Would you hug your fig leaves around you to cover the nakedness of your soul? Or will you come to Christ to be cleansed by His blood and clothed with His righteousness that He might present you faultless before His throne with exceeding joy?

There will be one day, says Christ, a great wedding feast. And all that come there will have on the beautiful white wedding garments—a picture of the righteousness of Christ. In the parable in Matthew 22:1–13, there came a man not wearing a wedding garment. And the king came out to look at his guests. His eyes fixed upon the one man there that had no wedding garment, and he said to him, "Friend, how camest thou hither? How dare you come into this presence dressed in such vile and foul rags?" Ah, but he had supposed that he was dressed in his Sunday best—all of his Sunday school deeds, his character, his morality, his money given to charity, his commandment keeping, his Golden Rule living—he thought that he was just the nicest dressed person there! Then the lights went on, and he saw himself for what he was—foulness from head to foot! And the command came down to that one who was speechless, "Bind him hand and foot, and take him away, and cast him into outer darkness; there shall be weeping and gnashing of teeth" (Matt. 22:13).

To what are you clinging? In what are you trusting? Your righteousness or Christ's? Your merit or His? We are justified freely by His grace through the redemption that is in Christ Jesus.

"Foul, [we] to the fountain fly: Wash [us], Saviour, or [we] die." Lord, enlighten our minds by Thy Spirit that we may see ourselves as we really are, despise our sins, trust not in our own righteousness, but flee to the cross. And embracing it may we be cleansed by Thy blood, O Christ, within, and clothed in Thy precious righteousness without, that thus we may be justified from all of our sins and be fit to enter eternal life. Through Thy blessed name we pray. *Amen.*

9

Sanctification

Sanctify them through thy truth: thy word is truth. And for their sakes I sanctify myself, that they also might be sanctified through the truth.

John 17:17, 19

Away with vain words . . . Christianity is life—not doctrine. . . . Our only creed is Christ. . . . Let us be done with dogma and go on to duty." Familiar words? Do you believe them? Millions have. And with such shibboleths as these, the axe has been laid to the root of genuine Christianity by Satan himself. "For as [a man] thinketh in his heart, so is he" (Prov. 23:7). If there is anything peculiar to the Protestant churches which emerged from the Reformation, it is this: All life must be grounded in truth. That which we believe is going to determine what we do, and the life we live will spring inevitably from the beliefs that we hold. This is why we are saved by faith, and faith is the belief of the truth and the reception of it as such.

Christianity, indeed, is not only life, it is also doctrine. It is a life that is produced by belief. Those who would castigate creed and dogma and doctrine should perchance take a look again at what these words mean. The word *doctrine* comes from the Latin word *docere*, which means "to teach." The word *creed* comes from the Latin word *credo*, which means "I believe." The word *dogma* comes from the Greek word *dokeo*, which means "to think." Therefore, a person who has no dogma, no creed, and no doctrine is a person who neither thinks, believes, nor teaches. But if you are going to think anything, believe anything, and teach anything, then, my friends, you need dogma, creed, and doctrine. This is the substance that forms the foundation of the Christian faith.

The problem with so many today is that they do have dogma, doctrine, and creed, but they are usually of their own making. They have mixed them up and brewed them in their own minds. The problem is not that they do not hold such, but that which they hold is corrupted by untruth and falsehood. This is the reason for the low state of morality and the apathy that is rampant in this country and the church today.

If we are going to have a vital life in the church, then that life must spring from the truth. Abraham Kuyper, the great Dutch theologian, gave this illustration: There was a time in centuries gone by when outside in the world there was only darkness and freezing cold, yet in the church there was warmth and joy and zeal, as people warmed themselves beside the fires of the truth of the Word of God. But those fires became corrupted with untruth. Slowly they dimmed and went out, and a chill settled on the church. Those inside became aware of their condition and their coldness, and they bestirred themselves to do something about it. There arose in their midst those who gave them an answer for their problem. "You see," they said, "you can get no heat from fires. The thing to do is to remove the fireplace entirely and create the heat in your own soul without the use of fire. Simply rub your hands together hard enough, and soon you will be warm." But the biblical answer is to light again the fires of truth. This is the prayer of Jesus Christ: "Sanctify them through thy truth: thy word is truth" (John 17:17).

We have come in our series of doctrinal studies to the doctrine of sanctification. This is an exceedingly important doctrine because it reaches us right where we are. This has to do with our Christian life as we are living it right now. There are many who have said, "Certainly this is such a simple doctrine that it could not be corrupted with falsehood. It is merely living the Christian life, so we need not worry about the doctrine of sanctification; let us have the fact of sanctification." But the problem is that today not one church member in ten has the foggiest notion of what the biblical doctrine of sanctification really is. This is the reason, I believe, there is so little true sanctification in the church today. Sanctification is a doctrine as well as a life.

What is the biblical doctrine of sanctification? With what does it deal? What is its nature? What is its origin? What are its means? Sanctification is closely related to the doctrine of justification, which we studied earlier. Since these terms are often confused, we need to distinguish them. Though they can never be separated, they must be distinguished. According to the Reformers, the confusion of the doctrine of sanctification and the doctrine of justification was one of the principal errors of the Church of Rome, which teaches that if we become sufficiently sanctified, we shall in the end thereby be justified. But the Bible teaches that we are justified first, and this results in our sanctification.

Let us look at these two terms and see if we can grasp the difference between them. First of all, justification is an act; sanctification is a process. Justification takes place once for all and is complete and perfect; sanctification is imperfect and is a long process that lasts from the beginning of the Christian life until the moment we die. Justification is something that is external to us; sanctification is something that happens within us. Justification, in its metaphorical sense, is the act of a judge (what a judge declares about us); sanctification is more the work of a surgeon (something done within us). Justification is something that is declared about us—that we are not guilty and are declared to be righteous; sanctification is something that is done to us.

Having now grasped these few distinctions between the two doctrines, let us further consider the difference and the purpose of these two works of God. Both of them have to do with two different aspects of sin, for according to the Scriptures, sin has two aspects. If you do not distinguish these in your mind, you will have great difficulty understanding Christian theology.

The first aspect of sin is what is known as guilt. Guilt is liability to punishment. I would not want you to confuse that with guilt feelings, which are played up so strongly in so many of our psychological writings today and strangely enough even by those who deny the reality of guilt. If a person breaks a law in the civil realm, he or she is now liable to punishment if caught. This is guilt. We who sin against the law of God are liable to punishment. The second aspect of sin is something within us, and that is corruption. Thus, the two aspects of sin are guilt and corruption. Guilt is outside of us (not guilt feelings). It has to do with our relationship to the law. Corruption is inside of us—our corrupt natures.

God is going to deal with both of these aspects of sin. He deals with the matter of guilt through justification. In the act of justification, the righteousness of Christ is imputed to us and we are declared to be righteous as far as our relationship to the law is concerned. This is done once for all. We do not grow in righteousness. We are no more justified twenty years after we have accepted Christ than we were the moment we accepted Him. We are given the perfect righteousness of Christ. We are clothed with the garment of salvation and covered with the robe of righteousness. But sanctification is doing away with our corruption. And this is done, not by the imputation of the righteousness of Christ to us once for all, but by the gradual infusion of the holiness of Christ into us. Both our righteousness and our holiness come from Christ.

Let us pause for a moment to see if we understand the difference between these two aspects of sin: guilt and corruption. Instead of guilt, what we need is righteousness in the sight of the law; and instead of corruption, what we need is holiness.

It is here that people have difficulty grasping the matter of holiness. Perhaps you might grasp it better if you thought of it in terms of this illustration. Is there anyone who doesn't know how it feels to unknowingly bite into an apple and find it to be corrupt? Perhaps the term *rotten* would be a little more familiar. This is simply to say that in the sight of God all of us are rotten apples. That is corruption.

If that doesn't jolt your sensibilities enough, may I point out to you that there is also another result of rottenness. If you leave a rotten apple around long enough, it will begin to have a strange odor. God says we are a stench in His nostrils. Now that's not very pleasant, but that is God's portrait of humankind. From the top of our heads to the soles of our feet, there is nothing but corruption within us. Therefore, we need the holiness of Jesus Christ. In English the word *holiness* comes from the word *whole*—wholeness, soundness, oneness. If anyone were able to make a rotten apple sound, that would be an amazing feat. We know how to make a good apple rotten, but how do we make a rotten apple good? Only God can do this. One reason that apples rot is that they are taken off the tree. You take any apple off a tree and leave it around long enough and it's going to get rotten. If we are severed from the Vine, we are going to become corrupt and rotten. Holiness is an attribute of God alone, and any holiness that exists in anyone or anything in this world exists only because it is related to God. The holiness of God has flowed into it in some way. The purpose and object of sanctification is to make us holy in the sight of God.

Having been justified, we are removed from our liability to punishment; we are declared innocent and not guilty. Having been clothed with the garments of Christ, we now need to become holy within. The Bible says that God is of purer eyes than to look upon iniquity, that all sin, whether it is in an unbeliever or a believer, is contrary to the holiness of God and is an abomination in His sight (see Hab. 1:13). He despises sin. The commandment of God to us is "Ye shall be holy; for I am holy" (Lev. 11:44). This is the matter to which sanctification addresses itself. God commands us to become holy. "Without holiness no man shall see God," is the teaching of the Bible. We are to perfect holiness in the fear of the Lord. If there is anything that the church of Christ needs today, it is a view of the holiness and majesty of God and a consequent view of His demands upon us that we are to be holy as He is holy. Are you holy?

"For all that is in the world, the lust of the flesh, and the lust of the eyes, and the pride of life, is not of the Father, but is of the world. And the world passeth away, and the lust thereof" (1 John 2:16–17). These are not of the Father. They are vile in His sight; they are rotten. And yet we live in such a rotten world. Those who come to see the glory of God will cry out in their anguish saying, "I am a man of unclean lips and I dwell in the midst of a people with unclean lips: for mine eyes have seen the King, the LORD of hosts" (Isa. 6:5).

What is your particular form of corruption? Is it the lust of the flesh? God calls us to holiness in body, mind, and spirit. Anything which is contrary—any rottenness, any corruption—God demands that it be replaced by that which is sound and holy. How many minds today are virtually pornographic? How about the body, which God commands be presented unto Him as a living sacrifice, holy, and therefore acceptable in His sight? Is your body holy? Or is it contaminated with all manner of vile deeds and habits? Is your spirit holy? What about the lust of the eyes (covetousness)? The Bible says that covetousness is a corruption in His sight. How about the pride of life? Vain ambition? Seeking to be better than our neighbors? Pride in our knowledge? Pride in our ability? The pride of life is another form of vile rottenness, says He who can say, "Learn of me; for I am meek and lowly in heart" (Matt. 11:29).

Without holiness, no one shall see God. Whence then are we to obtain this? Sanctification is not merely an effort on the part of Christians to live a better Christian life. In fact, sanctification is not really the effort of man at all; sanctification is the work of God. It is God that sanctifies. Salvation is of God, whether it be justification in the past tense, or sanctification in the present tense, or glorification in the future when the final vestiges of sin are removed. Salvation is wholly of God. It is God that sanctifies.

The agent of sanctification is not man but the Holy Spirit. It is the infusing of the holiness of Christ. There is no holiness in us. A rotten apple could jump up and down, bestir itself, clap its hands, and do whatever it wanted to, and it would still be nothing more than a rotten apple. And so there is nothing about ourselves that can make us holy.

This does not mean that we are passive in sanctification. We are passive in regeneration, but we are active in our sanctification, though it is still all of grace. We are to make use of the means of sanctification, which are the Word of God, prayer, obedience to all of God's commandments, the sacraments, and worship. The Holy Spirit takes our use of these means and makes them the method by which He sanctifies us. But let me remind you that you could read the Word of God until you were green in the face, and you could pray until your knees were worn smooth, and you would not be sanctified one bit if the Holy Spirit of God did not sanctify you. Therefore, you can see that there is the required instrument of faith to reach out and take hold of God. It is faith that looks unto the Spirit of God and cries out that God would make us holy, sanctify us, make us pure, and cleanse us from our sins.

There is the need of faith, realizing that we cannot sanctify ourselves, realizing that God demands holiness of us, realizing that we are incapable of producing it. Therefore, we not only make use of the means of grace, but we trust in the Giver of grace and the Sanctifier of people—the Holy Spirit of God.

Are you aware of your corruption? Does your heart cry out in anguish as you consider your inward disease? Are you growing in grace? Are you more faithful in your prayer life? If you would grow in sanctification, then make use of the means of grace. Start spending more time in prayer. Start seriously studying the Word of God. Determine that you are going to give yourself over to the new obedience and walk in all of the ways of God's commandments. Many a Christian is determined to walk in part of the ways of God's commandments and thus gets nowhere at all. Repentance requires determination after obedience on our part.

Would you know the holiness of God? Then you will have to know Him who is holy; for apart from Him, the thrice-holy God, there is nothing in this sin-tainted world but death and corruption. Draw near unto Him. Spend time unto Him. Reach out in faith unto Him. And you will come to know the blessings of God's holiness and the meaning of His sanctification.

O God, deliver us, we pray Thee, from a corrupted view of Thy holiness. May we never forget that Thou hast said, "Be ye holy, for I am holy . . . without holiness no man shall see God." For thou art the altogether holy one. O Lord, teach us to despise our sin and corruption, our vileness and rottenness, and may we reach unto Thee, O Thou Source of purity and holiness, that we may be healed and made whole in body, mind, and soul. We pray it in the name of Christ. *Amen.*

10

Adoption

For ye have not received the spirit of bondage again to fear; but ye have received the Spirit of adoption, whereby we cry, Abba, Father.

Romans 8:15

In the preceding chapters, we have seen how God revealed Himself through the Scriptures and ultimately in His Son. We have also seen that the central person about whom this revelation speaks is the Triune God: Father, Son, and Holy Ghost. We have seen that God is infinitely sovereign, in control of all things in the world from the greatest to the smallest. There is nothing that takes place that is not under His control. He firmly holds in His hands the reins of the world; kings and subjects do according to His bidding. Whether it be by His directive or His permissive decree, all things come to pass according to Him who has foreordained everything after the council of His own will.

We have seen that God, after determining to create the world, made man in a perfect, sinless state. He then placed him on probation and gave him one commandment that, if kept, would earn for him and all humankind eternal blessed-ness, bliss, and peace forevermore. But man, because of his fallibility and out of his own willfulness, chose to rebel against his Maker and thus plunged the whole human race into sin and earned for his posterity, not life and peace, but death and misery.

God could have let man go his own way and allowed him to face judgment and punishment. But in His infinite mercy, God determined to show favor and grace to His creation and offered humankind eternal life. He foresaw, however, that this offer would be spurned, for "there is none that seeketh after God . . . they are all gone out of the way" (Rom. 3:11–12). Left to himself, man's heart is at enmity with God. His mind neither understands nor appreciates the things of the Spirit.

Therefore, God decided to select from this mass of fallen humanity some whom He would determinately save. To this end, He predestinated a great mass of people out of every nation, tongue, and tribe to make them His children (see Rev. 5:9). He not only invites them, but He sends His Spirit to bring them irresistibly, invincibly, unfailingly, effectually unto Him-self, renewing their hearts and minds, quickening them from the deadness of their sins, and bringing them to Christ. Hav-ing been made willing by His grace, they come most willingly.

To provide this salvation for humanity, God gave His only begotten Son to die in their stead for their sins, to pay for their transgressions, so that God might show favor unto them and still remain the just Judge of all the earth. In His proper and appointed time, He sent forth His Holy Spirit to effec-tually call them, and by His Word and Spirit dead sinners leap to life, their minds quickened, souls renewed, wills changed and made malleable. After hearing God's voice and knock at the door, they say, "It is my Beloved; I will go and open unto Him" (see Col. 4:3). We have seen that after being given faith by God as a gift, man is also justified on the basis of that very faith so that all his salvation may be of grace. Salvation is of God. But the *ordo salutis*, or the way of salvation as it is divinely revealed in the Scriptures, is not yet complete.

In this chapter, I want to discuss one of the greatest doctrines of the Christian faith: the doctrine of adoption. This doctrine has been greatly neglected throughout church history. Luther had little to say about it, and Calvin ignored it almost entirely. The great theologian Jean Alphonse Turretin confused it with the second part of justification wherein man is clothed with righteousness and made righteous in the sight of God. To be made righteous in the sight of the law is entirely different than to be received into the house of the Father. We find that the well-known theologian Robert Lewis Dabney followed in the train of Turretin and made the same mistake. Even the great systematic theologian Charles Hodge omits it from the paragraph headings of his volumes. However, the Westminster Confession of Faith does contain a brief chapter on adoption.

Because it has been neglected, I think it is important that we rediscover this great doctrine. It is important, first, because it is of immeasurable solace to the saints of God when calamity overwhelms and tribulation comes in like a flood. What child of God has not turned to Him after losing a loved one? Is it not to our Father's home that our hearts turn when this earthly tabernacle begins to crumble and dissolve? This is what adoption is all about.

Secondly, it is important because it is a biblical doctrine— the great end to the doctrine of predestination. We are predestinated that we might become the adopted children of God. Adoption is the consummation, the ultimate blessing, of the Christian life.

Thirdly, it is important because it is the theological point of contact with this century's greatest heresy. It is said that every century has its own peculiar heresy, and this century has been no exception. Universalism is a doctrine that is spreading and being proclaimed forcibly and eloquently from many pulpits across our land, even when the creeds of the church explicitly deny it. It is the doctrine that says that some-how, somewhere, sometime, every one of God's creatures will ultimately arrive in paradise. It is a doctrine that utterly denies and abhors the biblical doctrine of eternal punish-ment and rejects the scriptural teaching that humanity could forever be separated from God. Yet the Bible plainly teaches, and Christian churches believe, that there will be those who will be forever separated from God. Jesus Christ Himself made it plain, "Enter ye in at the strait gate: for wide is the gate, and broad is the way, that leadeth to destruction, and many there be which go in thereat: because strait is the gate, and narrow is the way, which leadeth unto life, and few there be that find it" (Matt. 7:13–14).

The point at which universalism impinges upon the doc-trine of adoption is what is called "the fatherhood of God and the brotherhood of man." I suppose many Christian people believe the doctrine of the fatherhood of God and the broth-erhood of man to be biblical. This merely proves Hitler's dic-tum: Tell a lie which is big enough, tell it loud enough and often enough, and you can get most people to believe it. This is just what Satan has done at this point, and his success is notable. The concept of the universal fatherhood of God and universal brotherhood of man is utterly foreign to the Scrip-tures. It is only in the past fifty or seventy-five years that it has even been seen in theological writings. It is an utterly for-eign doctrine to older biblical scholars because it is com-pletely foreign to the Bible.

Jesus said, "Ye are of your father the devil and [his works] ye will do" (John 8:44). Paul says we were "children of dis-obedience" (Eph. 2:2). This is the state of the natural man as he is born into this world. He is a disobedient child of the devil, under the wrath of God. One family with one Father? Not at all! We must be translated out of the kingdom of dark-ness into the kingdom of God's dear Son. All sons of God? Listen: "But as many as received him [Christ], to them gave he power to become the sons of God" (John 1:12).

How can one become something he already is? Of course he cannot. "They which are children of the flesh, these are not the children of God: but the children of the promise are counted for the seed" (Rom. 9:8). "Wherefore come out from among them . . . [I] will be a Father unto you, and ye shall be my sons and daughters" (2 Cor. 6:17–18). No, the deception of the devil may be that all people are the sons of God and that He is Father of all, but this is not the teaching of the Scriptures.

To be perfectly accurate, let me point out that the term *sons of God* is used in Scripture three ways. First, when God originally made man, he was the son of God. This is his lowest concept. (That condition was utterly obliterated, as we shall see.) Second, there is the adoptive sense of all believers: "For ye are all the children of God by faith in Christ Jesus" (Gal. 3:26). It is only those who have faith in Jesus Christ who are the sons of God. And third, in its restrictive, single, unique sense, it refers to the Son of God, Jesus Christ Himself, who is the eternal Second Person of the Trinity and has forever been the Son of God.

Let us look at the beginning and see what happened. God made Adam as His son—perfect, without sin. But Adam was not only the son of God, he was also the subject of God and stood before God in both of these relationships. If we want to understand biblical theology, it is important to understand that Adam was not only son but also subject. He was a member of the divine kingdom, but also of the divine household. God, to him, was Sovereign and Lord; He was also Father and Friend. Adam was placed under probation in both of these relationships, both as a citizen of the kingdom and as a son of the Father. If he had obeyed, we would all have had an eternal citizenship in the kingdom of God and eternal sonship in the household of God. But rather, he sinned against the magisterial favor of the King and against the paternal regard of his Father. In one act, he sinned both ways. The result was spiritual death. This means that as a citizen he was outlawed, and as a son he was banished and disinherited. Therefore, all his children (each one of us born into this world) are born under the scowl of a righteous Judge and the frown of a benevolent Father.

This is man's condition. It is described succinctly by Dr. Robert Webb, who said concerning Adam and all of his natural children after their sin:

> There was, there could be, there ought to have been, but one denouement to such a situation—a child with a heart so perverted ought to have been excluded. God dismissed him. Today he has neither the right nor spirit of a child. He is legally disowned because he is morally bad. He is ungoverned, because he is ungovernable. He has thrown off his Father's authority, because he has cast away his Father's disposition. Moral gravitation has naturally and logically carried him into that fellowship where the outraged sensibilities of his Father have justly consigned him. Parental discipline has dealt with him according to the demands and desires of his own degenerate nature. He has been permitted to have his willful way; and the misery of his course will be the just retribution of his heady and impertinent career. He is a child of Satan; therefore a "child of wrath."

Now what does man need? He needs a twofold remedy for his condition. The exact status of fallen man is a proscribed citizen and a disinherited child. It means he must be restored to his legal citizenship in the kingdom of God and must be recovered into the bosom and household of his Father. This is his problem. What is its solution? This double solution is clearly stated in Scripture. On one hand, the problem of citizenship is dealt with by the doctrine of justification. In justification the transgressed law of God is fulfilled by Christ and the penalty paid by Him. Sinners are clothed in the righteousness of Christ and restored to the kingdom of God. Their sonship is taken care of in the doctrine of adoption whereby they are adopted into the family of God and restored to His household.

When we look more closely at the doctrine of adoption, we notice that it has some relation to the doctrine of justification. We also note that it has a relation to the doctrine of regeneration because the problem of adoption is twofold. The child must be restored not only to the filial position, but also to a filial disposition. The natural man must be given a filial nature, the nature of a child, because he has a spiteful attitude toward his parents. It is the attitude of teenagers who say to their parents, "I hate you; I never want to lay eyes on you again. I couldn't care less what you have done for me." But when such people are regenerated by faith in Christ, they are given a new heart and nature and are restored to the rights and privileges of the household of God. This is done by adoption.

Let us look carefully at the theology of the fatherhood of God and the brotherhood of man. Also let me state again that this is a new religion which is foreign to the historic religion of Jesus Christ. It's a religion of paternalism. I think it's interesting that universalism should rise in the twentieth century when we see the same thing happening in government. People want a paternalistic government and a paternalistic religion where they believe God is just naturally the Father of everyone. Such people say God created people because He was lonely. They fail to realize that God is the absolute, perfect Person; the three Persons of the Triune God have never been lonely. God did not create man because He was lonely; He created man for His own glory. People also fail to understand the difference between divine government and divine discipline, between the ruling of a Sovereign and the ruling of a Father.

And what are these differences? They are seen in many ways. For example, a sovereign-state ruler exercises justice and punishes the rebellious citizen, the transgressor of the law. A father operates on the basis of love and chastens rather than punishes his child.

The difference between punishment and chastisement is great. Punishment is retrospective—it looks backward to the broken law and is not done to make the criminal better. Rather, it's done because the transgressed law demands punishment. Chastisement is prospective—it looks to the future. It's given not for a broken law, but for the presence of a fault. It's to make the child better. An electric chair never made anyone better. It may make society better, since one of the reasons for justice is the protection of society; but the reason for chastening is to make a better child.

Further, the universalist denies the need of an atonement and reduces the Bible to the story of the prodigal son, where the father embraces the son without atonement or payment for his sins. But you see, that's the nature of fatherly discipline. All the father requires is repentance and evidence of a desire to do better in the future. So these people suppose this to be the way of salvation. They believe if a person merely repents and evidences that he will do better in the future, all will be well.

This is to suppose that a murderer given a life sentence could, after two days in jail, rattle the bars and say to the warden, "Warden, I've had a change of heart. You'll be delighted to know I'm sorry about the whole thing. I've decided I shouldn't have killed all those people. It just wasn't the right thing to do. Please tell the jailer to open the cage and let me out, because I'll never do that again." There's a difference between fatherly discipline, the practice of justice, and the penalty of the law!

The univeralist, therefore, fails to understand that God not only makes man a member of His kingdom, but also adopts him into His family. Both of these are found in Jesus Christ, who came not only as Servant, but also as Son. Jesus as the suffering Servant is subject to the King, obedient to God in all His ways. Jesus pays the penalty as the Servant, and thus God restores Him to His legal citizenship in the kingdom. Jesus is also the very Son of God because it takes the Son by filial obedience to restore the sinful, disobedient son to a filial relation. And so Christ, the suffering Servant and suffering Son, comes and provides for us not only our justification and restoration to the kingdom of God, but also our adoption and reclamation into the family of God. This is the great biblical doctrine of adoption.

We are bought into the family of God, given His name, and made heirs by an act of God's grace. We also have the promise that we have His Spirit put within us. He pities us as a Father, provides for all our needs, watches over us, defends us from our enemies, and one day will take us to that mansion in glory which He has prepared for us. How wonderful it is that because of the Spirit of adoption we can look up into the face of God, whom many fear, and say, "Abba, Father" (Rom. 8:15).

I once pointed out to a Jehovah's Witness that their *New World Translation* of the New Testament was not correct in including, scores of times, the word *Jehovah*, which does not appear even one time in the Greek text of the New Testament. This person responded by asking, "Why would God not use His name in the New Testament?" I cannot answer for God. Though I cannot for sure say why He did not do it, I can for certain state that He did not do it. I do have an idea, however, as to what the reason might be. Let me explain it by this story. When our little girl, Jennifer, was about five years old, she passed through a phase where she began to call her mother and me by our first names—Anne and Jim (since she had heard others do this). After a few weeks of this, I sat her on my knee and said to her, "Jennifer, darling, there are thousands of people in this world who can call me Jim, but there is no other person on this earth who can call me 'Daddy,' except you. And to you, Jennifer, my name is Daddy!"

So also God revealed His name in the Old Testament as Jehovah—the Ever-Living One. But in the New Testament, when we are given the Spirit of adoption and brought into that intimate relationship of children of God, we can look up into the face of our Father and say, "Abba," which is a diminutive of the Aramaic word for father and means Daddy!

Are you a child of God? Have you come to the place of receiving Jesus Christ? Can you say, "I'm a child of the King"?

"But as many as received him [Christ], to them gave he power to become the sons of God" (John 1:12). Beloved, now are we the children of God. In Jesus' name. *Amen.*

11

Assurance of Salvation

These things have I written unto you that believe on the name of the Son of God; that ye may know that ye have eternal life, and that ye may believe on the name of the Son of God.

1 John 5:13

Not long ago a radio announcer in Chicago took a survey in a train station. He asked about twenty-five or thirty people if they knew for sure that they were going to heaven. The result was interesting—a unanimous No. In fact, several became indignant and said, "Nobody can know such a thing as that!"

Contrast this with the statement by the great scientist Sir Michael Faraday, discoverer of magnetism, who on his deathbed was asked, "What speculations do you have about life after death?"

"Speculations!" he replied in astonishment. "Why, I have no speculations! I'm resting on certainties! I know whom I have believed, and am persuaded that He is able to keep that which I have committed unto Him against that day!"

This certainty of heaven is not only the possession of the great and wise of the world, but also of the poor and humble. An elderly Scottish woman who lay at death's door was visited by her pastor. "Sadie," he said, "suppose when you die God should allow you to perish. What then?"

"Well," she said, "that's up to Him. He will do what He will. But if He does allow me to perish, He will lose more than I; for though I will lose my soul, He will lose His honor, for He has promised me in His Word, '[He that] believeth in me shall never die'" (John 11:26).

An old fisherman, who lived by the sea, was asked by a friend if he still believed he was going to heaven. "Look out the window," said the fisherman. "Are the seven great stones still there?"

"Yes," said his friend.

"Is the old mountain crag there?"

"Yes," came the reply.

"Well," said the fisherman, "the mountains shall disappear and the hills shall be cast down, but the Word of God shall last forever" (see 1 Peter 1:25).

The Bible makes it plain that we can know what will become of us. But why is it that so many people today, in and out of church, do not know they are on their way to heaven? Because they *are not* on their way to heaven! Indeed it would be strange if God put into the hearts of people the assurance that they were on their way to heaven when in fact they were hastening into hell.

In a radio survey, a reporter asked people on what they based their hope of heaven. Without exception they said, "Myself, my efforts, striving, church going, goodness, character, morality, commandment keeping." No wonder people don't know or have the assurance. These answers are the antithesis of Christianity! All who are going to heaven know they are. Are you going there?

A few weeks ago I received a call from a young lady who was deeply perplexed. She had been going to a church whose modern minister was well informed about current events, but evidently quite uninformed about the eternal verities of the Word of God. He had completely confused her to the point where she didn't know where she was going or why. He declared that nobody could know they were going to heaven, and it was impossible for anyone to have a sudden or instantaneous conversion. "Salvation," he said, "is a long process and not something you can have overnight."

"What kind of church is this?" I asked.

"A Protestant church," she said.

"Well," I said, "I recommend this minister go back and check the foundations of Protestantism and examine its taproot."

I suggested he look at the life of Martin Luther, who struggled for years to earn his salvation. Finally, on his knees, crawling up the *sancta scala* (sacred stairs) in Rome while reciting his mumbled prayers, he was suddenly struck with the words, "The just shall live by faith!" (Rom. 1:17). We are justified by faith, not all these vain works! With the assurance of eternal life flooding his heart, Luther began the Protestant Reformation.

Consider John Calvin, the founder of the Presbyterian and Reformed branches of the Protestant world, who relates his conversion in one sentence, "God suddenly converted me unto Himself."

John Wesley, founder of the Methodist Church, said in his diary, "It was a quarter to nine and for the first time in my life I knew that I trusted Jesus Christ alone for my salvation. I felt my heart strangely warmed and knew that He had delivered me from sin and death unto eternal life." He didn't name the year, month, week, day, or hour—he named the minute! It was a quarter to nine! He came to know in a moment!

I told the young lady that the minister's denials were not peripheral matters, but struck at the heart of the gospel. They were perverting the Christian faith.

The Bible says eternal life is a free gift from God. It is unearned, unworked for, unstriven for, unmerited, undeserved. It's a gift completely paid for by Christ and offered by His grace. Then how long does it take to obtain this gift? You merely reach out and take it. "He [Jesus] came unto his own, and his own received him not. But as many as received him, to them gave he power to become the sons of God" (John 1:11–12). Eternal life is a gift that is received in an instant.

Did you receive a gift last Christmas? Did it take you twenty years to get it? Do you know whether or not you have it? So it is with eternal life! It is the greatest Christmas present God has ever given to the world. "The gift of God is eternal life through Jesus Christ our Lord" (Rom. 6:23).

The essence of Protestantism is this: Heaven is free and therefore we may know we have it. The Protestant faith does not keep people in fear of what will happen to them when they die. That is the essence of Romanism. The Council of Trent of the Roman Church says, "Let that man who says he knows he has eternal life be anathema." But the Word of God says, "These things have I written . . . that ye may know that ye have eternal life" (1 John 5:13). The Bible not only says you can know it, but commands you to know it: "Make your calling and election sure" (2 Peter 1:10). This is not advice; this is a commandment. Every day you fail to do that, you are sinning against God by breaking this commandment. "Make your calling and election sure." "These things are written that ye might [know]" (John 20:31). "We know that we have passed from death unto life" (1 John 3:14).

No, the Bible doesn't deal with question marks. The faith of the Bible is a stirring exclamation point! "For I know that my redeemer liveth" (Job 19:25). "I know whom I have believed, and am persuaded that he is able to keep that which I have committed unto him against that day" (2 Tim. 1:12). There is joy in such knowledge like nothing else can bring, because this assurance is the source of Christian joy. It is this kind of joy in our souls that puts spring in our steps and makes us sing songs as we walk down the street.

It was this joy that enabled blind Fanny Crosby to write, "Blessed assurance, Jesus is mine. O what a foretaste of glory divine!" No wonder many don't smile when they sing such a song. They are spiritually blind to the great truth it teaches! It is paganism that fills the heart with dark, doubting fear when death approaches. Christianity is a religion of assurance, faith, confidence, joy. The reason Christians can rejoice is because they know they are going to heaven. The apostle Paul says, "Rejoice . . . and again I say, Rejoice" (Phil. 4:4).

His heart burdened with sin, Charles Spurgeon sought for God as a young lad in London. For five years, he wandered from place to place seeking someone who could give him a word of assurance. He said he did not so much fear the wrath of God as he feared sin itself for what it was. He said, "If some preacher had told me to bare my back and with fifty lashes would earn eternal life, I would have instantly ripped the shirt from my back and said, 'Do your worst. Spare not the rod if it will bring peace to my troubled soul.' If they had told me to run a hundred miles barefooted, I would have started off immediately, if I could have gained eternal life. But to trust in Christ, rest upon His finished work, simply by faith take hold of Him, do nothing except believe and receive, this I knew not how to get hold of at all."

Then one day when he was but sixteen-and-a-half, still bound by sin, Spurgeon wandered into a little chapel. There were only twelve or fifteen people present. The regular minister was gone and an uneducated, unlettered layman got up to speak. He chose for his text these words: "Look unto me, and be ye saved, all the ends of the earth" (Isa. 45:22). He began in the simplest language: "There's not a hand that's lifted or a foot that's moved; there's not a thing that's done. Only a look, because there's life for a look at the Crucified One. The problem with many is that they look to themselves. As long as you look within yourself, you will never find the secret of salvation. 'Look unto Me,' says Christ. Not unto God the Father—that will come later; not unto the Holy Spirit—look unto Jesus who came from glory and died for our sins."

Suddenly the layman stopped, looked down, and saw young Charles Spurgeon. Pointing his finger at him, he said, "Young man, you're miserable. Further, you are going to be miserable forever unless you obey my text: Look unto Christ."

"And," said Spurgeon years later, "in that moment my soul was flooded with the reality of the grace of God. I looked unto the cross of Jesus Christ and saw there His hands pierced for my sins; I saw Him bearing the burden of my guilt upon His back; I saw the wrath of God that I deserved falling upon Him. Suddenly I realized that it was finished! It was done, the payment made, it was over, and I knew I had received eternal life. My soul was filled with joy. I could have danced all the way home. I could not restrain myself but to tell another one of the Jesus, blessed Jesus, whom I had found and who had found me."

Do you have that blessed assurance? It is the wellspring of all Christian motives for holy living. Unless you know you have eternal life, everything you have ever done for Christ has been a sin. I repeat: Unless you know that you have eternal life, everything you have ever done for Christ has been a sin—because your motive was wrong! If you don't know you have eternal life, everything you are doing is an effort to get eternal life, and thus your motive is gain and greed. But God in His mercy came down, incarnate in Christ, died on the cross, paid for our sins, purchased for us eternal life, and by His graciousness offers it freely to us as a gift. Faith is but the hand of a beggar reaching out to receive the gift of a King. The motive, then, for Christian living is not gain, but gratitude for the gift of eternal life. God begins by giving us everything!

Have you received eternal life? Or is death still for you an uncertainty—a leap into outer darkness? If so, I assure you it will be just that: outer, eternal darkness where there will be weeping and wailing and gnashing of teeth. But you *can know.* That doubt can be changed to singing and certainty that will bring forth joy and peace. Would you receive the gift He offers you? Would you take Him at His word? "He that believeth not God hath made him a liar; because he believeth not the record that God gave of his Son. And this is the record, that God hath given to us eternal life, and this life is in his Son. He that hath the Son hath life" (1 John 5:10–12). Do you believe it? Have you received it? Have you invited the Son to come into your life as Savior, Master, Lord? "He that believeth on the Son of God hath the witness in himself" (1 John 5:10). "The [Holy] Spirit itself beareth witness with our spirit, that we are the children of God" (Rom. 8:16).

And then, if you have done that, you can sing with real meaning: "Blessed assurance, Jesus is mine. O what a foretaste of glory divine."

12

Good Works

For by grace are ye saved through faith; and that not of your-
selves: it is the gift of God: not of works, lest any man should
boast. For we are his workmanship, created in Christ Jesus
unto good works, which God hath before ordained that we
should walk in them.

Ephesians 2:8–10

In this chapter, I want to discuss the place of good
works in the scheme of Christian theology. Is man
redeemed by his own works? Are we required to
do them, and do we have any?

As believers in Christ, we have been set apart or sanctified
unto good works (see 2 Tim. 2:21). From this we see that
sanctification is essentially the mortification of the old man
and the creation of the new. In discussing the work of sanctification in producing good works, we must remember that
sanctification is the work of God the Holy Spirit within us.
Sanctification is creating a new nature, a new heart, a holy
disposition. The soil of our own character, of our souls, is
changed; and holiness is implanted within us. Good works,
on the other hand, is something done by us. "This is a faith-

ful saying, and these things I will that thou affirm constantly, that they which have believed in God might be careful to maintain good works" (Titus 3:8).

While the work of Christ is vicarious, the work of the Holy Spirit is not. Christ does something for us, in our stead, in our place, as our substitute. He died in our place on the cross. The hope of our salvation is based upon the vicarious substitutionary work of Jesus Christ in our stead. The work of the Holy Spirit is not. He does not do something for us; He works in us. His work can never be counted as our own. He creates something within us, and He stirs us up to do something in response to that. This something that we do is called good works. Sanctification is something imparted to us. Good works are something taken from us.

Now what is a good work? There are three requirements of any work before it can be called good in the biblical sense. The first and most obvious is one many people seem unable to grasp. What is the most basic thing required of a work for it to be good? I have asked this question of dozens of people, including classes of elders and deacons I have taught. I had all sorts of answers, but the simplest and most obvious always eludes them. The first requirement for a work to be good is that it be commanded by God, that it be conformable to divine law. No matter how holy or zealous our inclinations when we decide to do something for God, if He has not commanded us to do it, then the good work is not pleasing to God. God says, "Who has commanded thee to do these things?" (see Acts 5:28).

Religions through the centuries have commanded people to do all sorts of human works that they invented as supposedly pleasing to God. But the only way to please God is to obey Him.

Philosophers have invented schemes to determine what is good. John Stuart Mill's famous definition was "that which does the greatest good to the greatest number." This is called utilitarianism, but it is not always true. Hitler was a utilitarian. Furthermore, it's often completely impossible to determine what will do the greatest good to the greatest number. Communists are sure they are doing the greatest good to the greatest number when they kill millions of people to make way for communism.

Some say, "Good is the thing which brings me the greatest pleasure." Others have said that good is that which is expedient; and if it seems to be expedient, it's good. There are others who say good is what they have learned from Grandpa. It's amazing how many ethical standards have been handed down from Aunt Susie, Mom and Dad, Grandma and Granddad. "As old granddaddy used to say. . . . Now that's what I believe and that's what I do." It doesn't matter that the Word of God contradicts it. Granddaddy did it that way, and that's the way it's going to be! This is making a god out of our grandparent. Every opinion of people must come under the scrutiny of God's Word. Only God, the absolute Lawgiver and Creator of this world, can determine what is good.

Therefore, we can begin by saying that the good person is the obedient person. People say, "Oh, he was such a good man. Of course he didn't go to church, read the Bible, or pray. He didn't do this or that. But he was a good man." That is not true! If he was a disobedient man by the biblical definition of that which is good, he was not a good man. A good person must first become an obedient person—obedient to the will of God—and the holy law of God is the divine transcript of the immutable and eternal will of God. Furthermore, the good person obeys out of love for God. "If ye love me, keep my commandments" (John 14:15).

The first aspect of a good work, then, is that it is something God has commanded us to do. Don't worry about this, because God's law, which rises up out of the trunk of God's basic will, branches off into the ten branches of the Ten Commandments and then contains thousands of boughs, smaller branches, and leaves, covering all aspects of human conduct. God has told us clearly in His Word what He wants us to do. Never in this life will we get through doing what He has told us to do, much less have to invent something He didn't tell us to do.

I am amazed at people who suppose a Christian is to have nothing to do with the law of God. This antinomian (against the law) teaching has clung to the church like a cancer for centuries but is completely contrary to God's Word. Jesus Christ fulfilled the law as a covenant of works and took the penalty of it, but the law of God still remains the only transcript of the immutable will of God. "He that hath my commandments, and keepeth them, he it is that loveth me" (John 14:21).

The second requirement for a work to be good is that it must be done from a heart purified by faith. Hypothetically considering any work by itself (for example, giving a thousand dollars to the poor) is one thing; but considering it in relation to the motive, object, or end of the person doing it, is another. We see that it's possible for us to do tens of thousands of things that God commands us to do without ever having done a single good work—because the good work must first come from a heart purified by faith. Jesus states this explicitly when He says, "A good tree cannot bring forth evil fruit and a corrupt tree cannot bring forth good fruit" (Matt. 7:18). It is impossible for the human heart in its natural, depraved, sinful state to ever bring forth anything that in the sight of God would be considered good.

The human heart must be purified by faith because "without faith it is impossible to please [God]" (Heb. 11:6). Faith is that which lays hold of the justifying and sanctifying grace of God. Faith brings the Holy Spirit into the heart to cleanse, wash, purify, and work within us those holy inclinations and dispositions to do things which are truly pleasing to a Holy God. Without the cleansing of the stream at its source, it can never bring forth pure water. A bitter fountain cannot bring forth sweet waters any more than a corrupt tree can bring forth good fruit. What does this mean? It means that unregenerate people (human beings as they are born into the world before receiving Jesus Christ as their Savior and before the Holy Spirit has created a holy state within them) can only bring forth evil fruit until God changes their hearts.

Therefore, the reason unregenerate people cannot get to heaven by their good works is not because they do not have *enough*, but because they don't have *any!* "For whatsoever is not of faith is sin" (Rom. 14:23).

The Bible says "the plowing of the wicked, is sin" (Prov. 21:4). Consider that devastating statement! This means a non-Christian farmer who rises before sunrise and goes about his duties, working in the fields while the blazing sun beats down upon his perspiring back, is sinning in the sight of God. Why? Because, even though God commanded man to work with his hands and earn his daily bread, his motive for working does not proceed from a heart cleansed and made holy. Therefore, his work is sin.

The same situation would apply to pirates who infested the islands off the Florida coast. A search into their activities might reveal many commendable things. They might have been nice to their wives and cared for their children. They might have been generous and worked diligently at their boats. They might have worked hard to plant and raise crops. Yet every seed they planted, every ear of corn they harvested, was part of the effort to gain more food, to gather more strength, to continue their willful rebellion against the authority of the United States. Therefore, they were guilty and the government could only ask them to surrender.

So the plowing of the wicked man is merely an effort to gain food, to gain strength, to continue his willful rebellion against the rightful sovereign authority of Jesus Christ. There are church members who diligently work or study, yet everything they do is sin because they are gathering more strength to continue their rebellion against Almighty God who commands us to lay down our arms and surrender to Him. A good work must proceed from a purified source—a heart cleansed by faith with a true love of God.

Not only must a good work be something that is commanded by God in His Word and come from a purified heart,
but it must also be done to the right end. This is the third
and last aspect of a good work.

At a "Men of the Church" picnic, one of the gentlemen
brought a magnificent archery set. I've never seen anything
like it, though not because I'm completely unfamiliar with
the sport—I used to enjoy it. (Before we were married I
bought my future wife just what any young lady's heart would
most desire—two archery sets! Do you think my motive was
right?) The set was beautiful—marvelous arrows, straight,
polished, and strong. But regardless of how magnificent the
bow, how strongly bent, how straight and powerful the arrow,
it would avail nothing at all unless the aim were right.

Do you see the point? It makes no difference how beautiful a deed may be in itself. It makes no difference how
highly polished, how magnificent and extraordinary, how
much effort and energy goes into the work. If its direction
is not right, it matters not at all, and the work is not good; it
is sin.

Suppose, while admiring the archery set, I had picked up
the bow and arrow and accidentally shot it into the heart of
one of my friends. This thing of beauty now becomes an
object of horror—an instrument of death. Unless our works
are directed toward the glory of God, they are not good.

What is the chief end of man? What is the purpose for man's
existence? Why are we here? What are we supposed to do?
What is the chief function of a can opener? It's to open cans!
We once had a can opener that was attractive. It had intricate
gears that would go around and around, but it wouldn't open
a can! And you know what happened to it? The garbage can!
That's exactly what God says will happen to us. God made us
for His own glory, and if we become useless and do not fulfill
the things for which we are made, then we will end up in what
He calls Gehenna of fire—the garbage heap of Jerusalem. We
shall go away into eternal fire (see Matt. 3:10).

The chief end of man is to glorify God and to enjoy Him forever. "At thy right hand there are pleasures for evermore" (Ps. 16:11). We are to enjoy and glorify God. The end of all our actions is to be the glory of God. The conscious, thoughtful, purposeful, directed end of our actions is always the glory of God. Any action which falls short of that glory is thereby not a good work and is sin. Abraham Kuyper says that the intention, direction, and aim of the heart is *everything* in what we do. The end and aim of all things must be the Lord God alone. We were created to glorify Him, and regardless of what the proximate aim may be, the ultimate aim of everything we do must be the glory of God.

We talk about self-denial, but the biblical concept of self-denial is to completely deny self not only in respect to people, but also in respect to God—to deny pointing our good deeds back to ourselves, to deny seeking praise for ourselves. Jesus condemned the self-righteous, "for they loved the praise of men rather than the praise of God" (John 12:43).

A young man once told me he couldn't see anything wrong with a person going out for his life's goal, seeking to be successful, to make a name for himself, to be famous, and to make money. But God says the essence of sin is for us to put ourselves in God's place and direct all our glory at our own egos, at our own selves. Satan said, "I will lift up myself into the place of God."

Abraham Kuyper illustrated this essence of sin by saying that every ship has a small, unseen object that controls its destination—the rudder. It doesn't matter how magnificently rigged the schooner may be, how full the sails, how rich and precious the cargo, or how streamlined the hull; unless the rudder directs the ship to its destination, it will end up on the rocks of disaster.

So it is with our good works. Beneath the waves of our lives, unseen by others, is a rudder that directs all we do. It either directs our works to the glory of God or turns them back to the glory of ourselves. We seek either the end of God's glory and magnificence or the end of our own advancement and praise. It matters not how fully rigged and magnificent may be the good works of our lives, or how precious the cargo of seemingly good works we carry, it's the rudder that makes the difference.

The great cry of the Protestant Reformation was *soli deo gloria*—solely for the glory of God. Thus every action of man must be solely for the glory of God. We are to win people to Jesus Christ, not merely so they may be saved or for us to be obedient, but rather that the glory of the majestic mercy of God may appear. These only are good works.

Again my question: Do you have a good work? How foolish for unregenerate people to believe they can buy eternal life and earn their way to heaven. Are we saved by these good works? Evidently not, because until we are saved, we do not possess one good work. "We are . . . created in Christ Jesus unto good works" (Eph. 2:10). Salvation is "not of works, lest any man should boast" (Eph. 2:9). It's a matter of the cart and horse. "Therefore by the deeds of the law there shall no flesh be justified in his sight" (Rom. 3:20). We are saved by faith in Jesus Christ alone—nothing else!

Are good works necessary to salvation? The answer is Yes, they are. They are the necessary consequence of our salvation. This is not only the answer of Scripture, but also that of the Apostolic Fathers and the Reformers (Luther, Calvin, Knox). It is the answer of the statements of all the great Protestant churches. It is the statement of the Westminster Confession of Faith. It is the Word of God: "Even so faith, if it hath not works, is dead [vain, empty, meaningless, nonexistent]" (James 2:17). As Martin Luther said, "People talk about being saved by faith plus good works. This is not true. Good works are the necessary consequence of our salvation. They are not necessary to be saved; they are the necessary result of our salvation and the evidence that we truly have faith." You could no more have faith without good works than you could have lightning without thunder or fire without heat. If we have a saving faith, we will inevitably have good works.

Luther also said that this faith is a divine work within us. Faith begets us anew. Faith creates us as new people and new creatures, renews all the various faculties of our being, and is constantly engaged in good works. Faith does not wait till the question of our works is asked but has already done good works and is constantly engaged in doing them. A person who does not do such good works is a person without faith.

The Westminster Confession of Faith says that we are justified by faith alone. This faith which justifies is never alone in the individual who is justified, but is always accompanied by the fruits which this produces in the life. Faith in Christ produces a life of good works. Therefore, those people who make a profession of faith and then sit down and do nothing for God, who have no service or good works for the Lord, vainly deceive themselves about being in a state of salvation and in God's favor—which hope shall perish with them!

Good works are absolutely the necessary result of a saving faith and are the only evidence of it. "For by grace are ye saved through faith; and that not of yourselves: it is the gift of God: not of works, lest any man should boast. For we are his workmanship, created in Christ Jesus unto good works, which God hath before ordained that we should walk in them" (Eph. 2:8–10).

O God, may we prove our faith by our works. May we examine our hearts. May Your glory be ever before us as our aim and goal. May all we do be done to Your glory and praise. We ask it in Thy blessed name, who, with the Father and the Holy Spirit, are the eternal and most Holy God, now and forevermore. *Amen.*

13

Perseverance of the Saints

Moreover whom he did predestinate, them he also called: and whom he called, them he also justified: and whom he justified, them he also glorified.

Romans 8:30

The question with which I would like to engage your thinking is, Can a Christian cease to be a Christian? Or as it might be otherwise stated, Can a person who has been saved ever be lost? Can a person who has been regenerated ever become unregenerated? Can one who has been translated into the kingdom of God's dear Son be translated back into the kingdom and family of the devil? Can a person receive eternal life and then go to hell forever? This is an important question because it has to do with an important aspect of our lives and speaks of our eternal welfare.

Let us look at the question historically and see what others have said about it. We might begin with the Roman Catholic

Church. Its answer to this is yes, a person may be a Christian and then cease to be one, may be saved and then be lost. Let us look next at the Lutheran Church for its answer. The Lutherans reply that a person may be saved and then may be lost. How about the group whose theology is known as Arminianism (the Methodist Church being the largest representative, as well as others, such as the Holiness and Pentecostal Churches)? This group's answer is an emphatic yes, a person may be saved and then lost.

What answer is given by the Calvinist to the question, Can a person be saved and then lost? To that question the Calvinist says no. Here we have a distinct tenet of the Calvinistic faith, for virtually all others have said that it is possible to be lost after having once been saved. Therefore, it is important for us to examine this carefully.

The perseverance of the saints is a doctrine that historically only Calvinists have acknowledged and that virtually all others have denied. I might point out that Calvinism is far broader than the Presbyterian Church as such, and that there are other denominations which would be classified historically as holding to the Calvinist faith. These would include historically all of the Reformed churches. The Anglican Church of England was historically Calvinistic; the Baptist Church was entirely Calvinistic; and to begin with, the Congregational Churches were all Calvinistic.

Many of these churches, however, have thrown out some of their beliefs and no longer hold to the Calvinistic faith but have gone over to that other doctrinal viewpoint that is widely held in Protestantism, namely Arminianism. According to this view, a person may be saved and then lost, and then saved again, and lost again, and this may happen hundreds of times until a person finally dies. Then the question is, In which condition did he die? In which state was his soul the moment that he passed from this world, since this will determine where he went?

Let us now note carefully the matter of definitions. I think it would also be well to notice what we are *not* talking about. If people don't understand what grace is, they are not going to understand what perseverance in grace is. If they do not know what a saint is, they are hardly going to understand the perseverance of the saints. Those who are not Christians suppose that eternal life is something that is to be gained by their striving to live a good life. They do not have eternal life; therefore, they have nothing that they could lose except the possibility of getting it. These people do not understand that the Bible teaches salvation by grace as a gift of God by faith in Jesus Christ. We are not talking about a person trying to live a good life in order to get eternal life. That is not Christianity in any of its forms. Since eternal life is a gift and is freely given by God's grace to those who will trust in the Savior, we are talking about whether God will give us the gift of eternal life and then take it back.

I spoke this week with a man who received Christ as his Savior and received the gift of eternal life. One of his first comments was, "Well, I hope that three weeks from now I'm still a Christian." Would God give him eternal life and then take it back? The Bible says, "For the gifts and calling of God are without repentance" (Rom. 11:29). His gift of eternal life and His grace and His calling unto salvation are not repented of by God.

Some people have thought this doctrine means that a person can profess faith in Christ, then live any way he wants, and forty years later die and go to heaven. Not at all! The name of this doctrine is the *perseverance of the saints.* It has been called many things by other groups, such as *eternal security,* or *once saved—always saved.* However, I think that the true theological name is the best, for it is carefully formulated. It is the perseverance of the saints. It is not the preservation of the professors of religion, but the perseverance of the saints.

You will notice we are talking about saints, about those who have been sanctified by God, those who are His own. The Westminster Confession states it succinctly in these words: "They whom God hath accepted in His beloved, effectually called and sanctified by His Spirit, can neither totally nor finally fall away from the state of grace but shall certainly persevere therein to the end, and be eternally saved." The Confession is speaking of those who have been regenerated by God, called by the Spirit, sanctified, and accepted in the beloved—those who are truly regenerated.

Notice too that we are talking about perseverance. The Bible says that those who persevere until the end shall be saved. It doesn't say that we may make a profession and then live for the world, the flesh, and the devil for years and then go to heaven. Only those who persevere till the end are those who are going to heaven.

The question is, Will we persevere to the end? There is no question that those who do not persevere to the end will not be saved. But can we persevere? Can we hold out? I am reminded of the alcoholic who for about the fiftieth time was signing the pledge to give up drinking. Someone said to him, "Now this time sign it and keep it!" And he said, "Keep it? Man, I need somebody to keep me!" This has been the cry of many a heart who knows its weakness and its frailty. We need someone to keep us. Thank God there is such a One. The Bible says, "[We are kept through] the power of God unto salvation" (Rom. 1:16). The omnipotent power of God keeps us and holds us in this salvation. If it were not for that, none of us would persevere for one day. This fact should not lead to pride, for true Christians know clearly how weak they are. It is not that we have any strength in ourselves, but that we will be helped by God and enabled by God.

Might I point out to you that unless we believe in the perseverance of the saints, we cannot know that we are going to heaven? We may know that we are presently in a state of grace, but we have no way of knowing whether tomorrow we might fall from that state of grace and utterly perish. Therefore, it is only those who hold to this Calvinistic and biblical doctrine who can say, "I know I'm on my way to heaven." There are many in those various communions that I previously mentioned who (though their churches officially don't believe in this) as Christians have rejoiced in their hearts that they have eternal life and that Christ will never let them go.

Can you say, "I know that I'm going to heaven"? Do you know that you are saved? Of course these are two different questions. Can you say, "I know that I have eternal life; I know that I'm in a state of grace"? If you cannot, then the subject we are discussing is of no value to you. You must first repent of your sins, cease to trust in your own good works, in your own strivings, and put your trust in Christ alone for your salvation. Then you can say, "I know that I'm in a state of grace. I know that I am forgiven." Then you can also come to claim God's promise that He will keep that which you have committed unto Him against that day.

We have noted that a person may partially and temporarily fall away, though not totally and finally. There are many examples of this, not only in the lives of those in Scripture, but also in church history. Peter fell egregiously into sin: He denied his Lord; he blasphemed. But because of the seed of God in his heart, because of the eternal covenant of grace, because God was holding him by the hand, because He had sworn that He would not forsake him, because he was sealed by the Holy Spirit, he was brought back and became a faithful servant, even though he partially and temporarily fell away. In the case of Judas, however, we see that there was no such thing. He did not have a new nature. He was not a true believer. In fact, Christ had long before said, "Have not I chosen you twelve, and one of you is a devil?" (John 6:70). And so Judas did not return but went out and committed suicide.

What shall we say then about the multitude of people who have professed faith in Christ and have shown an interest in Christ and in religion? There are some who will make a profession, who for a while will soar to the heights and will become exceedingly enthusiastic and zealous in the things of Christ. But then, either suddenly or slowly, they will fall away; their zeal is no longer there; they are not concerned with the things of God; they go through the motions and finally even that ceases. Their hearts become cold.

What shall we say concerning these people? Well, we do not have to conjecture, because the Bible teaches us plainly about them. In the second chapter of the First Epistle of John, we are told this: "They went out from us, but they were not of us; for if they had been of us, they would no doubt have continued with us: but they went out, that they might be made manifest that they were not all of us" (1 John 2:19).

Those who make professions do not necessarily possess what they profess. There are many hypocrites who outwardly may seem to profess an interest in the things of Christ, but inwardly their hearts are unchanged. Finally their true colors are manifested and the true nature and desires of their hearts come forth and they turn to the world, the flesh, and the devil. The proverb is true that says the dog returns to his vomit and the sow that was washed unto the mire (2 Peter 2:22).

Now notice carefully the words from our text: "Whom he justified, them he also glorified" (Rom. 8:30). Justification is the first act of the Christian life; glorification is the first act in heaven. Justification is the first thing that happens to Christians on earth. They are pardoned for their sins. They are accounted righteous in the sight of God. They are clothed with the righteousness of Jesus Christ. Glorification is the first thing that happens to Christians in heaven. Every last vestige of sin is removed. They are made absolutely pure and holy, fit to stand in the presence of God. "Whom he justified, them he glorified" (Rom. 8:30). Those that begin the Christian life on earth, end it in heaven. For we are kept by "the power of God unto salvation" (Rom. 1:16), the Bible tells us.

Jesus said, "My Father, which gave them me, is greater than all; and no man is able to pluck them out of my Father's hand" (John 10:29). I want to point out to you that there have been many efforts to try to circumvent the import of that passage. There are those who say that it could be the devil who could take them out. The Greek text simply says "no one"—it is not "no man" but "no one." There are others who have said, "Well, nobody can take us out, but we can take ourselves out." Are you not a man? Dare you say that you have the power to overcome the grasp of the Almighty God? No one can be taken out of His hand—that includes you. All the forces of hell and earth cannot get them out of His hand. Do you suppose that you can get yourself out? Do you suppose that you would ever really want to?

Someone asked a Christian, "Are you not afraid that you will slip through His fingers?" He replied, "Friend, I *am* one of His fingers!" Every true believer is part of the body of Christ.

Now, if we have something for a few weeks, or months, or years, and then we lose it and die and go to hell, we may call that which we had whatever we want, but one thing that we can't call it is eternal life. At best it was a temporary blessing. But Jesus said, "I give unto them eternal life." Furthermore, He went on to say, "they shall never perish." And should we receive eternal life and then perish, Christ is thus made a liar and God's Word is untrue. "I give unto them eternal life; and they shall never perish" (John 10:28).

Jesus went even further and said, "[They] shall not come into condemnation" (John 5:24). This is because we are not under the law but under grace. The law cannot condemn us because we are not under the law, but we are under a covenant of grace. Therefore the law can do nothing. "Who is he that condemneth? It is Christ that died, yea rather, that is risen again" (Rom. 8:34). There is none to condemn us because Christ has taken for us our condemnation already.

There are others who say, "Well, why does God give us warnings in the Scripture against falling away if we cannot fall away?" If it is true, as Charles Spurgeon said, that we can fall many times on the deck of a ship, but God will not let us fall off the ship, then why are we warned against apostasy? Why does the Bible say, "Take heed lest [ye] fall" (see 1 Cor. 10:12)? Why does the Scripture say, "I keep my body under lest after I have preached to others I myself should become a castaway" (see 1 Cor. 9:27)? One thing we need to note here is that God is keeping us. But how is He keeping us—by magic or by moral means?

Let me give you an example. I told my little daughter, Jennifer, who liked to get in the car when it was parked in the driveway, not to ever fool with the gearshift because that could release the gears and the car could roll down the street and be hit by another car and she could be killed. I severely warned her, "Never touch the gearshift." One day while out visiting, I was sitting in the living room and saw her get into the car, which was parked out front. She couldn't see me, but I was watching her. All of a sudden I saw the car make that little jerk it makes when it's just been shifted out of park into neutral. I leaped out of my chair and went flying out the door. I rushed to the car, pulled open the door, and snatched Jennifer out—at which time I forthwith gave her something which I hope will help to improve her memory.

Now let us look at that incident. Why did I tell her not to get into the car if I was going to rush out and stop it? Because I wanted to train her to do what she ought to do. The fact that I told her not to fool with the gearshift doesn't mean that I wasn't going to do anything else.

There is a hymn that puts it well: "And, behind the dim unknown, / Standeth God within the shadow / Keeping watch above His own." God keeps us by moral means, not by magic; so we have these warnings that are repeated in the Scripture. Furthermore, we also know that by our fall we can bring to ourselves grievous chastenings—as my little girl is now aware; she didn't get killed, but she did get chastened.

This is Paul's conclusion of the whole doctrinal matter: "For I am persuaded, that neither death, nor life, nor angels, nor principalities, nor powers, nor things present, nor things to come, nor height, nor depth, nor any other creature, shall be able to separate us from the love of God, which is in Christ Jesus our Lord" (Rom. 8:38–39). And so it is in coming to Christ. The Bible says, "Come unto me . . . whosoever will [may] come . . . believe on the Lord Jesus Christ and thou shalt be saved" (Matt. 11:28; Mark 8:34; Acts 16:31). It is as if it is all up to you, and that's all there is to it. But we know that behind the shadows in the dim unknown, there is Christ, who says, "All that the Father giveth me shall come to me" (John 6:37). None of those shall perish, for this is the Father's will. There is a God who has said that He has loved us from before the foundation of the world, that we have been pre-destinated eternally to be conformed to the image of His Son.

And so it is with the keeping. Outwardly, God says in effect, "Keep yourself. If you walk off the road, you are going to get hurt! Stay on the road. Walk in the narrow way" (Matt. 7:13–14). But behind the shadows there is the One who says we are kept by the power of God unto salvation; there is the One who says that He is holding us with His almighty hand; there is the One who has said that He will never leave us or forsake us; there is the One who has said that the gifts and calling of God are not repented of; there is the One who has said that those whom He has justified He will also glorify.

We can take Him at His word and rejoice not only that He has saved us but that He will keep us. We can say, "Yes, we believe in the perseverance of the saints." Consequently, you can say, "I know that I am on my way to heaven!"

Father, we thank Thee that eternal life is a gift given and unrepented of. We thank Thee that we can become Thy saints, set aside and sanctified through simple faith in Jesus Christ; that even right now we can receive Him into our hearts as our Savior and Lord. We can know that eternal life and salvation is all of grace; that it is all of God and not of man. Lord, we pray that Thou would save, that Thou would keep, that Thou would cause us to give ourselves wholly over to those means of our preservation: to the Word of God and to prayer, to service and obedience to Thee—lest we be deceived and supposing ourselves to be secured in carnal presumption, we should perish from the Way. In the name of Him who loves us and who gave Himself for us. *Amen.*

14

He Shall Come Again

And to you who are troubled rest with us, when the Lord Jesus shall be revealed from heaven with his mighty angels, in flaming fire taking vengeance on them that know not God, and that obey not the gospel of our Lord Jesus Christ.

2 Thessalonians 1:7–8

He shall come" is the unequivocal declaration of the oldest creeds of Christendom. It is in the Apostles' Creed, the Nicene Creed, the Constantinopolitan Creed, the Westminster Confession of the Presbyterians, the Thirty-nine Articles of the Anglicans, and the Augsburg Confession of the Lutherans. It is in all of the great creeds of Christendom. It is found in all of the systematic theologies, the lectionaries, and the hymnals of all of the Christian churches of history. It is part of the great faith of Jesus Christ! He shall come again!

The Old Testament distinctly prophesies it. Scores of passages in the New Testament expressly declare it. Jesus Himself told us unmistakably: "Hereafter shall ye see the Son of man sitting on the right hand of power, and coming in the clouds of heaven" (Matt. 26:64).

The apostles also say we are "looking for that blessed hope, and the glorious appearing of the great God and our Savior Jesus Christ" (Titus 2:13) and that "our conversation [our life] is in heaven; from whence also we look for the Savior, the Lord Jesus Christ" (Phil. 3:20).

In that day we are to be "unblamable in holiness . . . at the coming of our Lord Jesus" (1 Thess. 3:13). "We which are alive and remain shall be caught up . . . to meet the Lord in the air: and so shall we ever be with the Lord" (1 Thess. 4:17). "When the Lord Jesus shall be revealed from heaven . . ." (2 Thess. 1:7). "When the chief Shepherd shall appear . . ." (1 Peter 5:4).

The apostles declared that there would come scoffers who would deny His coming: "Where is the promise of his coming?" (2 Peter 3:4).

Christ averred, "Hereafter, shall ye see the Son of man sitting on the right hand of power, and coming in the clouds of heaven" (Matt. 26:64).

In the Apocalypse, the apostle John declared, "Behold, he cometh with clouds; and every eye shall see him, and they also which pierced him: and all kindreds of the earth shall wail because of him" (Rev. 1:7). "Even so, come, Lord Jesus" (Rev. 22:20).

This second advent of Christ is the great hope of the Christian. It is to be the final culminating point of history—the great climacteric of the ages. When the last page of the last volume of history shall have been written, there shall be the final exclamation point: Jesus Christ shall come again! He shall appear in all of His glory in the sky. And in that day the drama of the ages shall be brought to a glorious conclusion.

How will it be? How will He come? Well, let me say that the Apostles' Creed is an effort to unite Christians in those things which are most assuredly believed. Unfortunately, it is true that there have been those who have laboriously worked over their charts and have set their dates for the return of Christ. And others have divided the people of God endlessly on all of the minutiae which are connected to the second coming. But here I would like to fix your attention simply on that great central event which all of the body of Christ has confessed as part of their faith—He shall come again!

Let me say, first of all, how it will *not* be. The second advent of Christ is not the coming of Christ into our hearts by faith when we trust in Him for our salvation and receive Him as Lord and Master of our life. No. That is the spiritual coming. The other will be physical. The second advent is not Christ's pouring out of His Spirit at Pentecost, as is maintained by some who have tried to evade the clear teaching of Scripture. Nor is it our going to be with Christ at death, or Christ's coming in great cataclysmic judgments in the history of the world, such as the destruction of Rome. No. All of these events are quite diverse and different from that which is described as the second advent of Christ.

Just how will He come? I believe that five adverbs describe clearly that final denouement of history.

He will come, we are told, *bodily*. When Christ led the disciples up the Mount of Olives on that final day of His earthly pilgrimage, after He had proclaimed again the Great Commission, He lifted His arms in blessing upon them. As they beheld Him, He was taken up until finally a cloud received Him out of their sight. And two angels appeared to them and said, "Ye men of Galilee, why stand ye gazing up into heaven? This same Jesus, which is taken up from you into heaven, shall so come in like manner as ye have seen him go into heaven" (Acts 1:11). How did they see Him go? They saw Him go bodily, physically. And likewise Jesus Christ shall come again.

And if He comes bodily, then, secondly, He must obviously come *visibly* so that we may see Him with our eyes, even as Job so many centuries ago declared. The apostle John in the last book of Scripture attests to this: "Behold, he cometh with clouds; and every eye shall see him" (Rev. 1:7). Every eye shall see Him!

Someone has imagined that this is now possible because of television. But that idea is ludicrous. His coming could not possibly be missed. When Jesus Christ comes again in all the glory of His Father, He will eclipse the sun—and every eye shall see Him—not only we who are living but, as Paul tells us, even the dead shall be raised from their tombs. The sea will give up the dead that are in it; that crystal sarcophagus will reveal those who have long lain in the bottom of the sea. The cemeteries will be opened. Westminster Abbey will give forth its honored dead. The catacombs of Rome will disgorge their dead. The mummies of Egypt will be unwrapped and revealed. All of the dead of the ages will be brought forth.

And every eye shall see Him! Judas shall see Him. We are told that those that pierced Him will see Him. And all the kindred of the earth will wail because of Him. Come now, Judas! Now you know where He is. There He is in the midst of the air in all of His glory. Now run to the high priests and betray Him once more—for you know where He is. What is the matter, Judas? Will not your legs move? Come now, Caiaphas, tell us once more that it is expedient that this one man die so that the whole nation may not perish. Come! Tell us how we should take Him with rough hands and skewer Him to a cross. Or are your hands so busily engaged in blinding your eyes, blocking the bright effulgence of His glory, that you cannot look at Him? Come now, Pilate. Call for a basin to wash your hands and tell us once more that you will have nothing to do with this man. For no one can find any place where he will have nothing to do with this Man. Indeed, they shall call for the hills to cover them and the mountains to fall upon them to hide themselves from the face of Him that sits upon the throne, from the wrath of the Lamb. He will come visibly and every eye will see Him.

We can say, thirdly, that He will come *gloriously.* Someone once said to me, "I suppose that if Jesus Christ came again, as some people say He will, and were to walk around Fort Lauderdale or Chicago or London in a business suit, that we would probably take Him and crucify Him once more." How little he understood what the second advent of Christ really means. For Jesus will not come again in humility, in humiliation. He will come this time in glory with the power of His Father, with all of His mighty angels attendant, with ten thousand times ten thousand of His saints, with the sound of a trumpet that shall wake the dead, and with the voice of the archangel.

None will dare lift a hand against Him, for He will come, this time, undisguised. When He came before, He came fully disguised: the disguise seen by the Bethlehem caravansary; the disguise of the mausoleum in stone; the disguise of the seamless robe and the sandals; the disguise of the face, the voice, and the eyes. But this time He will come with His glory unsheathed—and people will see Him as He really is. His glory will eclipse the brightness of the sun. Ten thousand of the most glorious sunsets or sunrises will pale into insignificance when He shall come with a myriad of angels attending.

> Look, ye saints! The sight is glorious:
> See the Man of Sorrows now;
> From the fight returned victorious,
> Every knee to Him shall bow.

He will come again, gloriously with clouds, with mighty angels, in flaming fire, with a voice of the archangel, and with the trumpet of God. He will be the most glorious sight that humankind has ever seen.

Fourthly, He will come *triumphantly,* triumphant over His foes! Those that pierced Him shall wail because of Him. For Christians it will be a day of great rejoicing. But for those who have been unbelievers—when they shall see the glory of His power—then it shall be a day of great wailing. *Dies Irae*, day of wrath, a day of trembling when Jesus Christ shall come again. For the unbelievers, He comes "in flaming fire taking vengeance on them that know not God, and that obey not the gospel of the Lord Jesus Christ: who shall be punished with everlasting destruction" (2 Thess. 1:8–9). Oh, my friends, what if it were today? What if it were today!

Christina Rossetti, the poet, said that she was seated once in a large audience, listening to a great symphony orchestra that was playing magnificent music. And then, all of sudden, at an instant, every player—with concerted action—reached up and turned the page of his or her music. At that moment she thought, So will it be when the Lord Jesus Christ returns in glory! Every eye shall suddenly—in concert—look up, and every head shall turn to see the coming of the Son of Man. And in that day, how will it be for those that do not believe, for those who have never repented of their sins, for those who have ignored the invitation of His mercy? It will indeed be a day of great fear, terror, and anxiety for them when Christ comes triumphing over His foes. They will be destroyed with everlasting destruction!

How will it be for you? We should remember that though the second coming of Christ is certain, it is also uncertain as far as the time is concerned. For we know not the day or the hour. Though some have foolishly tried to set the date, Christ has made it clear that it is kept in His Father's power alone. We know not.

And so, fifthly, we know that He will come *unexpectedly*, in an hour that we think not. Suppose I were to ask you if you thought that Jesus Christ would come today? Have you thought about it since you awakened this morning? You would probably answer no. And yet it should be a source of anticipation and expectation. We should say, "Come, my beloved, come. May this be the glorious day—the day of grad-

uation, of coronation, when we shall see Thee face to face."
It could be today!

Since you do not expect Him to come today, then this day
becomes a good candidate. It could be now. All of your
plans—your carefully laid plans for what you are going to do
next week, next month, next year, the next decade, your plans
for retirement—may all disappear in an instant should Christ
appear today. Unexpectedly, He will come. Like a thief in the
night, He will come.

Archibald MacLeish gives us a poem which describes the
end of the world in a most interesting way, in a most incon-
gruous way. For he sees the end of the world from the per-
spective of those who are witnessing a circus.

> Quite unexpectedly as Vasserot as
> The armless ambidextrian was lighting
> A match between his great and second toe
> And Ralph the lion was engaged in biting
> The neck of Mme. Sossman while the drum
> Pointed, and Teeny was about to cough
> In Waltz-time swinging Jocko by the thumb—
> Quite unexpectedly the top blew off:
> And there, there overhead, there, there hung over
> Those thousands of white faces, those dazed eyes,
> There in the starless dark, the poise, the hover,
> There with vast wings across the canceled skies,
> There in the sudden blackness, the black pall
> Of nothing, nothing, nothing—nothing at all.

What was there? He doesn't say! I think perhaps that he
didn't know. But we know, don't we? We know that in that
day when the stars shall fall as lead from the sky, and the heavens shall be rolled like a scroll, that there in "the canceled
sky," in the deepening hole that once was a universe, shall
appear the Son of Man in all of His glory. He shall come!

How will that day be for you? Will it be a day of keen antic-ipation? Of welcomed delight? Or will it be for you a day of dread and foreboding, a day of unutterable horror, of unspeakable terror, of indescribable alarm? Does it cause your heart to blanch with fear, to start back, to stand aghast, to tremble, and to cower? It all depends on whether Jesus has already come, by His Spirit, into your heart to redeem you, to forgive you, to make you His own, to embrace you in His love, and to forgive you for all of your sins.

Has He come into your heart? Have you opened the door of that heart and said, "Come, Lord Jesus, there is room in my heart for Thee"? If so, then that will be the day of days—the day of delight. You will see your Beloved, your long-sought Beloved, face to face.

But if you have continued impenitently in your sins, if you have been satisfied with only nominal Christianity, if you have been satisfied to have your name upon the roll and not Christ upon the throne of your heart, if you have rejected Him, if you have spurned the invitation of His gospel—then for you it will be the fulfillment of the worst of all your nightmares. For in that day, suddenly, the great day of grace shall close as a huge steel vault door closing forever—closed and ended—for all eternity. And you will have nothing to look forward to but certain judgment and condemnation.

But now, at this moment, the day of grace is still open, and the word of welcome still goes out. Oh, I would that the over-arching heavens could be made into a great crystal bell and that all of the myriad of stars could be welded together into one silvery tongue that would swing back and forth until at last it would ring against that crystal bell, and its sound would reverberate through all the cosmos until it set your soul to thrilling with the word: "Come!"

But if you still have not opened your heart on that day, then it will be as though all of the great guns and the great artillery, the sixteen-inch guns and the great cannons all together were to discharge simultaneously with one thunderous, reverber-

ating boom, and the voice would roar throughout your soul:
"Go!"

It is a simple arithmetical problem, a problem of division: the dividend, eternity, over the divisor, two choices (heaven or hell) equals the quotient, the unalterable destiny of your soul.

$$\frac{\text{eternity}}{\text{choice}} = \text{unalterable destiny}$$

Are you really a Christian? You know how you can tell, don't you? If you really belong to Christ, then right now you can pray from your heart this prayer, which concludes the canon of Scripture: "Even so, come, Lord Jesus." Come quickly!

The Holy Spirit

Jesus answered, Verily, verily, I say unto thee, except a man be born of water and of the Spirit, he cannot enter into the kingdom of God.

John 3:5

I once saw a great machine that almost filled a huge room. It was moving mightily with thousands of parts whirling and turning out its product. But all of a sudden it stopped! People began to scurry about, trying to fix it. The problem? Very simple. Someone had disconnected the power source, and all of that massive machinery was of no more use than a pile of junk. And so it is with our Christian lives: Unless we have the power of God, all that we know and all that we have learned will mean nothing. Our lives will be impotent, filled with discord and strife instead of the joy and peace and love of Christ. These come with the power, and the power comes from the Holy Spirit.

In this chapter we deal with that portion of the Creed which states, "I believe in the Holy Ghost." I have discovered from a personal survey that a large percentage of the people of America are confused as to just who Jesus Christ is. They think Him to be a great teacher, a great example, a marvelous exemplar; but only a minority of those surveyed understood that He was, indeed, God incarnate. If there is confusion concerning who Jesus Christ is, there is even more confusion concerning the Holy Ghost. The very words themselves cause many people to wonder, Did we not learn as children not to believe in ghosts? A ghost! Isn't that an apparition of the departed dead? And yet we are talking here about a living, vivifying spirit. Of course, *ghost* is simply an old English word for *spirit*. The words are synonymous.

Some of the old English books on the Christian life talk about sanctification and speak of improving your "ghostly" life. I am sure that today, if somebody saw a book on how to improve your ghostly life, they would think it was something out of the occult. The books were talking, of course, about our spiritual life. "I believe in the Holy Ghost," or the Holy Spirit.

Let's think about the Holy Spirit by trying to answer three questions: Who is He? What does He do? How may we experience the blessing of the Holy Spirit?

First of all, Who is He? Or should I say, What is it? I have noticed that a number of people, when referring to the Holy Spirit, refer to an "it." That is not surprising, seeing that virtually all of the cults deny that the Holy Spirit is a personality, a person. They all declare that He is an "it." This is most vociferously maintained by Jehovah's Witnesses, for example, or Christian Scientists, or Unitarians. They all agree in denying that the Holy Spirit is a person. Some of them will say boldly, "Show me in the Scripture where it says that the Holy Spirit is a person."

Shall I show where it says that the Holy Spirit is a person? It says it nowhere at all! But before the cultists become too ecstatic over that, let me also mention that nowhere does it say in the Bible that the Father is a person. You may look in vain for any statement that says that the Father is a person.

And yet, the attributes of personality are everywhere ascribed to the Father.

The same thing is true of the Holy Spirit. All of the attributes of personality are ascribed to the Holy Spirit—for example, intellect, emotion, volition, mind, heart, and will, and along with these, the ability to communicate and to act.

The Bible refers to the mind of the Spirit. If the Holy Spirit were merely a force, as the cultists maintain, if He were no different, as they say, than such forces as gravity or magnetism or electricity, then how could we possibly speak of the mind of the Spirit? Did you ever hear of the mind of gravity? The idea is absurd!

Furthermore, Scripture says that the Holy Spirit knows with His mind. In fact, it says that no one knows the deep things of God except the Spirit of God. Not only does the Spirit of God know, but He also foreknows the future. The Bible tells us that the Spirit will tell us of things that will come to pass. So the Holy Spirit evidently has intellect and mind.

What about emotion? The Bible says that we are not to grieve the Spirit of God. Did you ever hear of magnetism or gravity grieving? The idea is ludicrous! Furthermore, the Bible speaks of "the love of the Spirit." Now, if the Spirit has love and the Spirit can be grieved, then the Spirit obviously has emotional qualities.

How about volition or will? The Holy Spirit said, "Separate me Barnabas and Saul for the work whereunto I have called them" (Acts 13:2). The Holy Spirit willed that Barnabas and Saul should be set apart for the work to which He had called them. The Holy Spirit forbade them to go into Asia. Rather He led them on another course. The Holy Spirit clearly has volition, will, and therefore He can act. And He does in many ways, as we shall see.

Furthermore, it is obvious that with these attributes the Holy Spirit communicates. He takes the things of Christ and tells them to us—reveals them to us. The Holy Spirit speaks and hears. The Holy Spirit, therefore, has all the attributes of a person; the Holy Spirit is a person. Of that there can be no reasonable doubt.

What kind of a person, then, is this Holy Spirit? The Bible makes it plain that He is a divine person. Again the cultists will rise up and demand, "Where does it say that the Holy Spirit is God?" In Acts chapter 5 when Peter is speaking to Ananias and Sapphira, who withheld a portion of that which they claimed to have given to the Lord, Peter says, "Why hath Satan filled thine heart to lie to the Holy Ghost?" (v. 3). And then he says, "Thou hast not lied unto men, but unto God" (v. 4). To lie to the Holy Ghost is to lie to God.

Therefore, it is clearly seen in Scripture that the Holy Spirit is God. He is a person, the Third Person of the Godhead. We might note that in the Apostles' Creed there are three paragraphs. The first paragraph deals with the Father ("I believe in God, the Father Almighty, maker of heaven and earth"). The second deals with the Son ("and in Jesus Christ, His only Son, our Lord"). The third begins with an affirmation of our belief in the Holy Spirit ("I believe in the Holy Ghost"). We sing the *Gloria Patri*, "Glory be to the Father, and to the Son, and to the Holy Ghost." In the Doxology we sing:

> Praise God, from whom all blessings flow:
> Praise Him, all creatures here below;
> Praise Him above, ye heavenly host;
> Praise Father, Son, and Holy Ghost.

Praise whom? Father, Son, and Holy Ghost. The entirety of Christian worship is built on the concept of the triune God: Father, Son, and Holy Spirit.

What does the Holy Spirit do? His works are manifold indeed. To begin with, there is credited to His work the creation of our world. Remember that the world was without form and void until the Holy Spirit, the Spirit of God, brooded upon this waste and transformed that chaos into cosmos, into an orderly system, into the beautiful world we see today.

Secondly, we see that the Holy Spirit is responsible for giving us the Scriptures. "All scripture is given by inspiration of God" (2 Tim. 3:16). It is given by the Holy Spirit. The Holy Spirit caused the apostles and the prophets to write those things that God would have us receive, so that we may know that these are the words God has given—having been inspired by the Holy Spirit of God in a unique way in which nothing else has ever been inspired. As John Calvin said, "We may receive the words of the Holy Scriptures as if they dripped from the very lips of God."

Thirdly, the Holy Spirit is responsible for bringing Christ into the world. The Spirit came upon Mary and caused Jesus Christ to be conceived in her womb.

Fourthly, notice that at Pentecost the Holy Spirit brought into existence the Christian church. We see that the Holy Spirit is responsible for the creation of the world, of the Scriptures, of the incarnation of Jesus Christ, and also of the church. These, indeed, are mighty works which are attributed in Scripture to the Holy Spirit.

Furthermore, there are other works that the Holy Spirit does personally in our lives. The Holy Spirit is responsible for regeneration; that is, we must be born of the Spirit. Jesus Christ said, "Ye must be born again." Except we have been born of the Spirit, we shall in no wise enter the kingdom of God (see John 3:5, 7).

How tragic it is that so many millions of people in this country have been satisfied merely to have their names on a church roll and to be baptized or confirmed. Yet they have never experienced the transforming, regenerating power of the Holy Spirit, which alone can make them acceptable for admission into heaven. It is only when we repent of our sins and receive Christ as Lord and Savior of our lives that we are renewed by the Holy Spirit of God. The Holy Spirit is not only the regenerator of humanity, but He is the sanctifier as well.

There are many emblems in the Scripture of the Holy Spirit: the dove of peace as the Spirit brings the peace of God which passeth understanding; the emblem of water as we are washed by the Holy Spirit; the emblem of wind as the Holy Spirit blows and renews and cleanses; and the symbol of fire as the cloven tongues of fire sat upon the disciples at Pentecost. The Spirit purifies us. If we are ever to see God, we must have a pure heart, the Bible tells us. There is so much sin in the best of us—so much iniquity in all of us—that we need the purging, purifying power of the Holy Spirit to cleanse us in our lives.

In 1665 the Great Plague had London in its grip; and everywhere throughout the city, people were filled with panic and fear. The germs continued to spread unabated, hiding in all sorts of dark corners, only to break out and destroy more and more lives. Then suddenly and unexpectedly London caught fire, and the fire spread until the entire city was consumed in a great conflagration. Though the buildings were destroyed, the raging fire brought an end to the plague—the unclean germs were purged by the fire.

And so it is in our lives. The fire of the Spirit needs to purge our hearts of sin. Only the Holy Spirit can take away all of the dregs of sin in our lives and cleanse us—from lascivious thoughts, from evil deeds, from lust and impurity, from lying and cheating, from hostility and animosity, from envy and jealousy, and from rancor, bickering, and strife. Only the Spirit of God can take these things away. We need to call upon God daily to have that work done.

Further, the Spirit of God is the One who brings power to our lives. He is the Spirit of power, the Scripture tells us. How we need that power in our lives! How many Christians seem impotent to serve God, impotent to witness effectively for Christ. How many have never brought another living soul to Christ.

A minister was sitting on a trolley car years ago, and he noticed that when the motorman moved the handle a little bit, the car would start slowly forward. When he moved it more, it would go more rapidly. That would be easily understood if the trolley were powered by a gasoline engine. But he thought that with electrical power, all of that energy should surge into the engine at once, driving the trolley car at full speed the moment the trolley came in contact with the wire. He thought there should be no halfway in between.

So he asked the motorman about it. In reply the motorman said, "When I push this, the gripper grips the wire; but it does it ever so gently and only a little of the power flows into the machine. But when it grips it tightly, then the full power flows into the trolley car and it goes faster." He said, "We call the gentle grip 'skinning the wire.'"

The minister thought, I have several thousand members in my congregation who are just "skinning the wire." They just barely have enough power to inch along in their Christian lives. And they never accomplish anything for Jesus Christ.

My friend, what have you accomplished for Christ? You may be moving toward the end of your life, but what have you accomplished for Christ? Is there one living person that today is alive in Christ because of you?

The Holy Spirit also gives us the fruit of the Spirit: love, joy, peace, longsuffering, gentleness, goodness, faith, meekness, and temperance (see Gal. 5:22–23). That fruit comes only from the Spirit of God.

How is it in your heart? How is it in your home? If there is love and joy and peace, then the Spirit of God is filling you. But if there is bitterness, rancor and strife, hostility and envy, then the Spirit of God is not there. How we all need to see the Spirit of God flowing through us and producing that beautiful cluster of fruit in our lives!

The Spirit of God also is the One who gives us assurance. It is by the Spirit of God that we know our adoption. By the Spirit of God we know we belong to Him. By the Spirit of God we can say, "Abba, Father." It is the Spirit that witnesses to our spirit that we are the children of God. Do you have that assurance in your heart today?

It is the Spirit of God who also guides our lives and leads us. The Scripture says, "For as many as are led by the Spirit

of God, they are the sons of God" (Rom. 8:14). How wonderful it is to know that there is someone who is willing to
lead our lives! So many times we don't know what to do or
where to go or which way to turn. When we yield ourselves
to the Holy Spirit, He has promised to lead us.

You can go off on a trip to Europe somewhere and try to
make it on your own. You may not speak the various languages;
you may not have reservations when you get there; you may
not know how to get to the train station; you may not know
when your next flight is leaving; and you may be confused. Or
you can engage a good travel agent to lay out the entire itinerary for you. Then you will know that wherever you go, your
hotel has been planned, your flight has been planned, and your
train has been planned. Everything has been arranged.

So it is with the Holy Spirit. We can commit our lives to
Him, and He will plan our itinerary through this world. Some
Christians are blindly staggering around, not knowing where
they are going. They have never, by faith, committed their
lives to the Holy Spirit. "As many as are led by the Spirit of
God, they are the sons of God" (Rom. 8:14).

Finally, the Holy Spirit testifies of Jesus Christ. Jesus said
that when the Spirit of truth comes He will not speak of Himself, but He will testify of Christ.

Dr. Manford Gutzke used to say, "You can always tell a
church or an individual that is filled with the Spirit of God.
How? Because of the fact that he is speaking, or that church
is speaking, much about Jesus Christ." And he added that you
can always know that if a church or an individual is speaking
all of the time about the Holy Spirit, then that person or
church is not energized and motivated by the Holy Spirit of
God. For the Holy Spirit speaks not of Himself but testifies
of Me, said Jesus (see John 15:26; 16:13).

How may we experience the Spirit's blessings? The Bible
says, be filled with the Holy Spirit: "Be not drunk with wine
wherein is excess; but be ye filled with the Spirit" (Eph. 5:18).
I have in the past used this illustration: We are leaky vessels,

like sieves; though we may be filled, we leak out that power; we need to be refilled. But I have come to see that that is not really the best analogy for being filled with the Holy Spirit. The Holy Spirit is a person, and you cannot have part of a person in you and have part of that person leak out of you. That is not the case at all.

I think a better illustration is this: Suppose you have a house without air-conditioning; so your house is hot inside, stuffy and musty and moldy and mildewed. It is just miserable to live there! So you break down and buy an air conditioner, a wall unit that you place in the central room in your house. Then cool air flows into that room. It flows through the doorways and into all of the other rooms. It cools your entire house, assuming the unit is adequate for the job. Everything is delightful!

But then you begin to close the doors in one room after another. And you leave them closed. The first thing you know, you have only one room that is cool, and all of the rest of the house is hot and stuffy and mildewed again. Miserable!

That is the way it is with the Spirit of God. It is not that we need more of the Spirit; it is that the Holy Spirit wants more of us. It is that we have confined Him in one small room of our lives, and there are parts of our lives that we are withholding from Him. We need to throw open the doors and let the Holy Spirit take over our minds, our habits, our hearts, our affections, our will, our speech, our feet, our hands, and all else that we are—and then let the Holy Spirit have control of all of our lives. This is what we need if we would be filled with the Holy Spirit and have every part of our being know the power and joy of the Holy Spirit. How can that be done?

First, we must confess our sins, the Scripture says. All of the sins! Confess all of the doors that have been closed to Him in all of the areas of our lives: our marriage relationship; our relationship with our parents, our children, and our friends; our relationships in our business, including our honesty and our personal relationships; our sex lives. Whatever the problem may be, we need to confess that sin.

We need, secondly, to repent of it—to determine by the grace of God to turn from that sin and follow Christ.

Thirdly, we need to ask God to fill us with the Holy Spirit. Jesus said, "If ye then, being evil, know how to give good gifts unto your children, how much more shall your Father which is in heaven give good things to them that ask him?" (Matt. 7:11). We need to ask God to fill us with the Holy Spirit. We are not asking Him to send the Holy Spirit if we are already a Christian, but rather to fill every part of our being with Him.

Fourthly, we need to believe that God will do just what Christ said—that the Father will give the Holy Spirit to them that ask Him. We don't need to wait for some ecstatic experience from God. It is the same as when we accept Christ; we must place our trust in Jesus Christ and take His word: "He that believeth in me already has eternal life." We believe His promise, and we go out and live by that promise. The same thing is true with the Holy Spirit. We need to believe that God has filled us with His Spirit when we have asked Him after having confessed and repented of our sins.

Fifthly, and last, we need to go out and live, knowing that we are empowered by the Spirit to go out and serve Christ. We are not given the Spirit merely for our own enjoyment or ecstasy, but that we might be servants of Christ and that we might glorify His name and build His kingdom on the earth. Knowing that we have that power, we then need to go and live with that power, exercise that power, and thus be a faithful witness for Jesus Christ and serve Him through His church.

May Christ grant you that fullness of His Spirit as you seek it from Him, and may you determine this day that you are not going to live just "skinning the wire," but that you are going to seek the fullness and power, the love and joy and peace that only the Holy Ghost can give you, so that you can say, in truth, from the very bottom of your heart, "I believe in the Holy Ghost!"

The Most Unpopular Subject in the World

And whosoever was not found written in the book of life was cast into the lake of fire.

Revelation 20:15

After a long, fatiguing day on a lecture trip to Pittsburgh, I flicked on the TV as I came into my hotel room. I was looking forward to a few moments of relaxation before turning in.

The program happened to be an interview talk show, and as my mind tuned to the discussion, I suddenly realized that over nationwide television the subject of the program was wife and husband swapping. The husband and wife being interviewed were obviously "swingers" and belonged to a group by the same name. After presenting views supporting their immoral lifestyle, the couple invited the audience to question them.

For the most part, the questions were pragmatic (wife and husband swapping didn't seem a practical way to run a marriage), but as each questioner presented an opposing view, the swingers demolished them with, "You're being too puritanical," or "That's mid-Victorian!" And they weren't fazed by a weak question about how they thought God viewed their lifestyle.

Later, as I reflected on the program, it became apparent to me again that humankind will wax worse and worse when God is left out of life. I was also reminded of Paul's statement in 1 Corinthians 5:1. What had been publicly aired on national TV was not even spoken of among the Gentiles! I realized afresh that all people need to understand that the Scriptures teach there is a hell.

I know many ranters, ravers, and demagogues have made the biblical doctrine of hell exceedingly distasteful. Some preachers have even spoken with apparent glee about the everlasting damnation of the wicked. I believe this to be truly sad, because whenever we talk about hell and those who go there, we must understand that they are real people with real flesh and real blood. Therefore, we must talk about hell with great sobriety and even tears, realizing it is what each of us deserves. Romans 3:10 says, "There is none righteous, no, not one."

Yet most people outside of Christ dismiss the concept of hell. The thought of endless and infinite misery so paralyzes their minds that they refuse to think about it. Others simply say, "I no longer believe in hell; it's too old-fashioned," which is like someone forming a society where all agree that Australia doesn't exist. But the reality of Australia will not change no matter how many people say it isn't there. In the same way, God and His Word are not affected by whether people believe in Him. A majority never rules His Word out of court. The tragedy is there are millions of people in hell today who, while on earth, closed their minds to its reality.

Frequently people will tell me they believe in heaven but not hell. When I ask how they know there is a heaven, most say, "I haven't given the matter too much thought—I just feel there is."

Feelings, of course, are most unreliable. The only way any of us knows about heaven is because God in His love tells us about it in His Word. People who confess that they believe in heaven but not hell fail to realize that God reveals both in the Bible. The same Scriptures that make known the glories and felicity of heaven also make known the terrors and awfulness of hell. There is no logical consistency to accepting heaven and denying hell.

Let us now, without being overwhelmed by our fears, take a rational and intelligent look at this matter. After repeatedly listening to a man punctuate his phraseology with *hell* one day, a friend of mine finally said, "Say, you seem to know a lot about hell. Is it because you've been there, or because you're going there?"

Taken aback, the man said, "Well, I suppose I'm going there."

"You know," said my friend, "you don't have to."

That, of course, is what the Bible is saying to us: "You don't have to, you know!"

However, it's a psychological fact that people suppress the thing they fear most. I am convinced that the person who fears hell most is the person who most vehemently denies its existence. But my word to you, and the word from Scripture, is that no one need cringe in terror worrying about whether he will go to hell.

I once asked three people what they had thought about hell before they became Christians. Their responses were identical: "I didn't like to think about it. But when I did, it was a most frightening prospect because I thought I might go there. I didn't know exactly what I had to do to get there, and I didn't know exactly what I had to do not to get there. I tried not to think about it."

I then asked what their thoughts and emotions were since their conversion. One said, "I am only afraid of it when I think of others. My fear is for them, not myself."

"Why are you now not afraid?" I asked. "Don't you believe it exists?"

"Yes," said all three. "We believe hell exists. But we're not afraid because we know we're not going there!"

This is an intelligent response to God's warning from Scripture. After warning us about hell, God doesn't leave us there. Rather, He shows us a way of escape. God says that when we by faith enter into a personal relationship with Jesus Christ, we are immediately saved from the penalty of hell (see John 3:18). From that moment on, throughout the rest of our lives and into eternity, we have the assurance from Scripture that we will never see hell.

If we have never entered into a personal relationship with Jesus Christ (even though we may have been church members for years), then we have reason to fear hell.

Let me repeat! People who refuse to believe in hell, or who think that denying its existence will make it go away, are deceiving themselves. Jesus Christ Himself, more than any other person in Scripture, talks about the awful reality of hell. But when Jesus speaks about hell, He doesn't speak to frighten. Rather He speaks to warn and offer Himself as the alternative to hell.

Sometimes people ask if the Scriptures talk about hell as an actual place. Indeed the Bible does. Look at some of the descriptive terms used:

> everlasting fire, prepared for the devil and his angels (Matt. 25:41)
> hell fire: where the worm dieth not, and the fire is not quenched (Mark 9:47–48)
> the lake which burneth with fire and brimstone (Rev. 21:8)
> the bottomless pit (Rev. 9:1–2)
> outer darkness (Matt. 8:12)
> [where] there shall be wailing and gnashing of teeth (Matt. 13:42)

It's a place where one cries, "I am tormented in this flame" (Luke 16:24). It's a place where "the smoke of their torment ascendeth up for ever and ever: and they have no rest day nor night" (Rev. 14:11).

In each case, all the Greek words used mean "everlasting, unending, eternal." They are the strongest words found in Greek for "never-ending duration."

The great A. A. Hodge said that all the great church fathers, Reformers, and biblical scholars, with all of their dictionaries, lexicons (both Hebrew and Greek), commentaries, and systematic theologies, concur that the Scriptures teach an endless punishment of the finally impenitent, and this in spite of a tremendous human desire in the opposite direction. So state all the creeds of the Presbyterians, Episcopalians, Lutherans, Methodists, Congregationalists, Roman Catholics, Greek Orthodox, and all the historic churches of Protestantism. Indeed, it is a mock charity that would encourage the impenitent to suppose there is any chance that God does not mean what He says.

There are those who try to create a divinity from their own minds and inflate it with their own conjectures. At best, their god becomes a wishy-washy idol without holiness, justice, or righteousness.

Those who suppose that God is too loving to ever punish sin do not know the God who has revealed Himself in Scripture. Those who also suppose that man is too good for such a fate do not know the heart of man as it is revealed to us in the Bible. But those who realize that God is holy, and that man is depraved, his heart unclean, realize that their hope lies in the death and resurrection of Jesus Christ. For on a cross outside the city wall of Jerusalem, the Son of God endured the wrath of His Father for those that would trust in Him.

I am convinced that the only way people will appreciate the biblical teachings on hell is to come to know in their hearts that they will never go there. Our Lord said that there is a broad way that leads to destruction, and a narrow way that leads to life (see Matt. 7:13–14). There is a Book of Life, and those whose names are in it will go into everlasting bliss. Those whose names are not found written in the Book of Life will be cast into the lake of fire (see Rev. 20:15). God has set His seal to it. His Word is true.

Is your name in that book? Are you on that narrow way that leads to life? Do you want to know God's way of escape?

Our hope is simply this: Christ died on a cross and we who trust in Him may by His grace go to heaven.

Have you by faith laid hold of Jesus Christ and invited Him into your heart? Have you repented of your sins? The promise of God is, "Whosoever was not found written in the book of life was cast into the lake of fire" (Rev. 20:15).

For those of you who have never accepted Jesus Christ into your life and want to, why don't you pray these simple words: "Heavenly Father, this day I embrace Your Son, Jesus Christ, as my personal Savior. I take into my own heart the One who came that I might live. I repent of my sins, which are many. Therefore, by faith I claim and believe the promise that he that trusts in You shall not come into condemnation but is passed from death unto life (see John 5:24). I rejoice that by Your grace I shall never see the bottomless pit and outer darkness. I thank You, Father, because now that I have taken Christ as my Savior, I shall, in the moment of death, be transported into paradise to be with You forever and ever." *Amen.*

Father the great purity of Your holiness stands in stark contrast to our sin. In our heart of hearts, we know none of us is righteous. O God, may we this day behold the Lamb of God, which taketh away the sin of the world (see John 1:29). Help us to know that the only way of escape is through a personal response to God's love in providing His Son, Jesus Christ, to die on the cross for the punishment we condignly deserve.

Father, if there are those whose hearts are still not right with You, I pray the Holy Spirit will incline them to repent and turn to Jesus, who stands with hands outstretched. *Amen.*

Heaven, the Life Hereafter

In my Father's house are many mansions: if it were not so, I would have told you. I go to prepare a place for you. And if I go and prepare a place for you, I will come again, and receive you unto myself; that where I am, there ye may be also.

John 14:2–3

God has created us for eternity. Yet most of us act as if He had created us merely for this life. In centuries gone by, it used to be said of some people that they were "too other-worldly"—too heavenly minded. This is certainly not something that can be said about many people today, for we live in a time that is so this-worldly, a time when people have all of their attention fixed on the world, the flesh, and the devil. The result is a society that is falling apart as everybody rushes to get more of that which satisfies the flesh. The people are like those whom Paul described when he said, "Whose end is destruction, whose God is their belly" (Phil. 3:19).

I believe that a healthy antidote to the cancer that is eating away at our society today would be a little healthful other-worldiness. If heaven is our home, if heaven is our destination, if heaven is the greatest thing that we can ever contemplate, how much time do we spend in thinking about it? It might be an indicator of whether or not we are going there—because those that are have a foretaste, an earnest in their hearts now; and those that are not, probably never give it a thought.

Heaven! What is it? Well, it's a major theme of the Scriptures. It's mentioned five hundred and fifty times in the Bible by that name alone. It is also called by many other names. It is the better country that the prophets sought after. It is called not only a country, but also a city, "a city which hath foundations, whose builder and maker is God" (Heb. 11:10). It is also called a house: "In my Father's house are many mansions." Furthermore, it is a real locality. Jesus said, "I go to prepare a place for you" (John 14:2).

There have been those who have talked about the heavenly city of Jerusalem and have said, "My, if that were actually a picture of heaven, we'd be so jammed up together that we wouldn't have space to turn around! Just imagine all of the people of heaven in one little city!" There have often been those who have scoffed at the Word of God; their problem has been that they have never really examined it carefully. In Revelation 21:16, we read of the city which lies four square, a city which was measured at twelve thousand furlongs long and twelve thousand furlongs wide. Now a furlong is an eighth of a mile, which means that this is a city which is fifteen hundred miles long and fifteen hundred miles wide— a city as long as from Florida to Maine and from New York to the Mississippi River. That's a pretty good sized city! That would be a megalopolis of the first order.

Imagine what this city would be like, because it is not only twelve thousand furlongs wide and long, but it also twelve thousand furlongs high, according to this passage—for its height and length and breadth are equal. The Empire State building has just over one hundred stories. This is a city that if it had stories—not of merely nine or ten feet in height but a commodious fifteen feet in height—would have 528 thousand stories! And on each of these stories there would be 2250 thousand square—not feet, but miles!—for a grand total in all of this city of 1 trillion, 188 billion square miles!

Now the department of eugenics has estimated that since humankind first began on this planet until today, there have lived approximately thirty billion people. One mathematician did a little figuring and came up with the fact that this would mean there would be 198 square miles for each family in this Holy City—if everybody who ever lived went there! And Jesus said there would be few that find the way and many that go to destruction (see Matt. 7:13–14). If even half the people made it, there would be about four hundred square miles per family—a good sized piece of real estate, as anyone can attest. I think that ought to be enough space for you to turn around! I wouldn't want to press that place that "eye hath not seen, nor ear heard, neither hath entered into the heart of man [what] God hath prepared for [us]" (1 Cor. 2:9) into any straightjacket of human words. I am sure that all of these descriptions are merely symbols that stir up our imagination but cannot begin to describe the beauties of that better country which God has prepared for us.

Heaven! Do you think about it much? Some people ask, "Where will it be?" Let me say this: Heaven is a real place, for Jesus said, "I go to prepare a place for you" (John 14:2). The Greek word for place is *topos* from which we get *topography* and *topology*—the writing and study of places. It is not a state of mind, nor is it here on this earth now; though some people say we have our heaven or hell now. But Jesus said, "And as it is appointed unto men once to die, but after this the judgment" (Heb. 9:27)—and then comes heaven or hell. It is after this life. Where is it? Now any high-school astronomer will tell you that if you look up into the sidereal heavens, you will find they are everywhere filled with sparkling galaxies, except in one place. Directly overhead to the north there is a great vast blackness which the most powerful of our telescopes has not been able to penetrate.

Of course we know that there was a Russian cosmonaut who went into space, and when he came back he assured us that there was neither a God nor a heaven. Recently he took a far longer trip, and when they lowered his body into the grave, many Russians cast fir branches in after him (the fir branch is a Russian symbol of immortality). Atheists? May I point out that Kosygin cast one also. The cosmonaut knows better now. But just think! He had gone up and taken a look, and God wasn't there! But where did he look? Imagine the billions of galaxies the size of our Milky Way (which has billions of suns in itself) and in this one small galaxy known as the Milky Way (millions of galaxies are far larger) there is a third-rate little star called *sun*, and that sun is invisible from much of our own galaxy. Around that little tiny sun there rotate nine planets, all of which are invisible from our nearest neighboring star. Around one of the smaller of those planets there circles a moon, so close as to be indistinguishable even from other planets in our own solar system. Somewhere between the moon and our earth, and so far closer to our earth as to be practically crawling on its surface, there went out a little Russian cosmonaut to examine the cosmos! And he found that God was not there! This reminds me of the little child, sailing his little boat around his bathtub, coming to the conclusion that Africa really isn't there, because it's not at this end of the bathtub, and it's not at that end of the bathtub!

John said he saw the Holy City descending out of heaven as a bride adorned for her husband (see Rev. 21:2). The great Dr. Charles Hodge of Princeton, the orthodox of the orthodox, has stated that it has been the consensus of orthodox theologians that the final abode of the redeemed after the judgment will be not only in heaven, but also on the new earth. John says there will be a new heaven and a new earth (Rev. 21:1). This earth will be purged by fire, reconstituted, glorified; and it seems that the dwelling place of the redeemed will be throughout the entire universe, which will be delivered from the bondage of sin at that time. How great will be the intellectual stimulation of inhabiting a sinless universe, which is now beyond our comprehension in its magnitude.

What will it be like? First of all, we will not be there as any Casper-the-ghost type, sitting on a cloud playing a harp. Occasionally, I talk to people who say they are not interested in going to heaven. When I hear a statement like that, I can conclude either (1) that those people do not believe there is a heaven, or (2) that they are so intolerably ignorant, so sluggish of mind and intellect, that it would be amazing if they could be interested in anything more than their own navels. Because if there's anything in this world that is deserving of human interest, it is the greatest thing man has ever conceived of: the paradise of God. If people should be wholly taken up and their interest consumed with the pathetic things of earth, which are twisted and distorted with sin, how infinitely more interesting will be the new heaven and the new earth.

We will have glorified bodies. Our senses will be enlarged greatly in their capacities. Already we know that compared to some of the other creatures in this world we are almost blind, deaf, and dumb. What will it be like then, when we are released from the bondage of sin? If we can hear beautiful music which causes our hearts to thrill now, when we are limited to a tiny, narrow wedge of the spectrum of sound, what will it be like when our ears are opened so that we may hear all of the vast harmonies of heaven? Right now we are almost blind when compared to the telescopic and microscopic sight of some birds. We can hardly see at all, and yet what will it be like when our vision is such as it will be in perfected bodies?

Beyond that, there is the infinite continuous progress of knowledge. Moral perfection does not do away with progress. There is such a thing as progress in perfection. Adam was perfect, yet he was not omniscient. He did not know all things, and he grew in knowledge. Jesus was perfect, and yet the Bible says He also grew in wisdom and in knowledge. So also we who now know in part shall then know in full. How wonderful it will be to begin to use some of the capacity of the human mind, which in the state of sin remains about ninety percent unused—even by the greatest genius that has ever lived. What a tremendous intellectual adventure it will be!

Then there will be the exemption from all sorrow. As Dr. Charles Hodge tells us, "What is it that takes away the joy of this life? Whatever it is, it will be gone then." For many it will be pain. It comes and disturbs their sleep. It knocks upon the door uninvited and unwelcomed as an intruder. It slips into the crevices of their bones. It throbs and beats and aches. How many there are who, if they could only be delivered from pain, would feel that they had entered into paradise already. But there will be no more pain there. "Neither sorrow," the Bible says (see Rev. 21:4). That pain of soul. How many people have had the joy of life sucked out of them by the sorrow of loss of a loved one. Their hearts are deflated, and it seems as if life will never have joy again. There will be no more sorrow then, nor will there be death, for there will be the continued enjoyment of all the blessings of heaven.

Also there will be no more sin. We don't realize that sin is what really takes away the joy of living. What a blessed fellowship—what a blessed communion there will be with the saints when there is no more sin, no more selfishness, no more anger or temper, no more pride or deceit, no more walking in darkness covering up the real intent of the heart. But there will be pure and perfect love. What a communion of souls and hearts as they are outpoured to one another in the great adventures that stretch before us forever in heaven.

Of course there will also be the outward and external beauties of that place. I was in Oregon, and how magnificent is that country with its beautiful mountains jutting into the sky. If this world under the burden of sin can show us something of beauty, what is this but crumbs off the table compared to that indescribable beauty that will exist in the paradise of the infinite God.

There will be the security that it shall never be lost. Whatever you have in this life and wherever you dwell, in South

Florida with all of its loveliness, or in the Swiss Alps, or wherever you might be, if you have all the wealth that one could want and the most beautiful of possessions, you will know that one day all of these are going to slip from your grasp. There is that dread of loss that old age brings, when so many people live in constant anxiety concerning their loss of all things. There will be here eternal security—the continued and never-ending enjoyment of all good forever. This will be the blessing of heaven.

There will be a blessing of reunion there also. I remember a touching story concerning Tony Fontaine, whose beautiful voice has lifted the hearts of many. His mother and father were devout Christians who worked in poverty-stricken areas for Christ. But their own child rebelled and wanted nothing to do with their disciplined life and their love for Christ. He was going to sow his wild oats and seek fame and fortune in this world with the talent that God had given him, but which he seemed to think was of his own making. He set out for Hollywood and became famous, and all the time his mother prayed for him. Night after night she would anoint her pillow with tears for her boy Tony. She grew old and sick, and Tony still did not come to Christ. Finally she died and left her son still unsaved.

Sometime later Tony was again confronted with the gospel. By the providence of God, he was brought to the cross, and he embraced the Savior as his own. He committed his life, his soul, his talent, and his all to Christ, and has since used his voice to change many a life.

One day while he was singing out on the West Coast, a woman came up to him (he had told his life story and had mentioned his mother) and said, "I'm leaving this week, and I'd be glad to carry a message to your mother if you'd like."

He said, "I—I thank you, but you didn't understand me. My mother is dead."

This elderly woman said, "Oh, yes, I understood you perfectly. But you see, I'm going where she is, and I'd be glad to carry a message to her if you'd like."

He stopped and thought, and said those words which he has sung so often, "Tell my mother I'll be there, in answer to her prayer. Tell my mother, tell my mother, I'll be there." Sometime later he learned that this lady died that very week, and I'm sure that the message was delivered.

What a blessed time of reunion that will be. One man said he really never understood what Jesus meant by treasure in heaven until he had lost a child. When that treasure had been deposited in heaven, he said, "Ah, my heart is there now. How real heaven became for me." Jesus said, "Where your treasure is, there will your heart be also" (Matt. 6:21). How blessed will be the reunions in heaven on that day. It is a place where there will be no more good-byes—only hellos.

The real question is not, Has a place been prepared for us? but, Are we prepared for that place? Will your name be called? Will your name be found written there?

The battlefield was strewn with bodies. The surgeon had done his best, and now he sat down for a moment of rest. Suddenly one cried out, "Here!"

The surgeon leaped up and ran to him and knelt at his side and said, "Yes, son, what can I do for you?"

The soldier opened his eyes, surprised, and said, "Nothing. They're calling the roll in heaven. They just called my name and I answered."

Will your name be found in the Lamb's Book of Life? You can have heaven there only by having it here. Life eternal is in Jesus Christ, and those who have received Jesus Christ here are those who will enter into life there. Christ said, "I am the way . . . no man cometh unto the Father, but by me" (John 14:6). Christ is life—life abundant and life eternal—and those who receive Him into their hearts as Lord and King and Saviour and Master are the ones that are going to be there. Will you be among them? Have you received the King of heaven as the King of your heart?

If you are going to heaven, there is one way that you can tell: You know it. For these things are written "that ye may know that ye have eternal life," the Scripture says (1 John 5:13). If you don't know that you are going to heaven, my friend, you're not—because if you are, you know it. God does not give His greatest gift without giving some assurance of its possession. Have you received Christ? Is He your all in all? Is He the One in whom you trust alone, or are you still resting on the poor and pitiful rags of your own righteousness? Can you sing, "Blessed assurance, Jesus is mine! Oh, what a foretaste of glory divine!"?

I am going to heaven. This I know. I do not deserve it, I never have, and I never will. But by the pure, unmerited grace of God, through the cross of Jesus Christ my Savior, I am going to paradise forever—and ever—and ever—and ever. Are you?

O Lord, for those who yet walk in darkness, staggering through the blackness of this world on their way to an eternal death, may the light of life shine upon their hearts; may they see their sin and their hopelessness. May they look into the face of Christ upon the cross and know that for this cause came He from heaven; for this cause laid He aside His glory and became incarnate in human flesh. For us and for our sin He died that the penalty might be paid—that the gift of God which is life eternal might be given. Lord, may they this hour believe. May their hearts this hour cry out, "Lord Jesus, I open the door. Come, Thou who are light and life and peace and joy. Come and bring with Thee Thy heaven. Dwell in my heart by faith. I receive Thee. I trust Thee. I commit myself unto Thee. Take me and make me Thine own, that I may love Thee now and love Thee forevermore." In Thy lovely name. *Amen and Amen.*

18

The Bible

In the beginning was the Word, and the Word was with God, and the Word was God.

John 1:1

Our Lord Jesus Christ said, "Sanctify [change or transform] them through thy truth: thy word is truth" (John 17:17). We are changed, our lives are transformed, by the truth of God. The truth of God is living, vital, and life-transforming; and it is vitally important, especially in this day of confusion, this day of ignorance concerning the things of God, that Christian people be well established concerning the truth of God's Word.

I talked with a young lady recently, and after ascertaining that she believed the Bible to be the Word of God, I said to her, "Tell me, what would you say to people who asked you to prove that the Bible is the Word of God? What would you tell them?"

She thought about that for a little while and said, "I wouldn't know what to say to them."

162

You say that you believe that the Bible is the Word of God. Is this simply some blind belief, some leap into darkness, some wish being the father to the thought? Or is there any substantive proof, any demonstration of the fact that the Bible is, indeed, the Word of God? I wonder how many of you would know what to tell a person who said, "Show me why you believe that this book is inspired by God. There are many books that claim to be inspired; there are many books that have been taken to be inspired revelations. How do you know which one is the truth?"

I was told that the book *Dust of Death* by Os Guinness pointed out that the great intrusion of oriental religions into America in recent times is possible because people do not have a grasp of the meaning of divine revelation. They do not understand what the Bible teaches about the nature, the uniqueness, the once-for-allness of the revelation that God has given to us in the Scripture. Therefore, they go after any sort of experiential or mystic type of experience that they think is going to give them some contact with God.

How do you know that the Bible is the Word of God? That is a good question to face when we are approaching any branch of human learning. It is what is known as the *epistemological question*. Epistemology is the study of how you know something. It is the science of knowledge. How do you know? That is the epistemological question. How do you know the Bible is the Word of God? How do you know that a prophet is sent from God? The Bible answers those questions very clearly.

Let us examine the matter. We note that the Bible explicitly and repeatedly claims to be the Word of God. It claims to be a revelation from God Almighty to mankind. Now that may not seem strange or even relevant to some, but I would point out that many of the scriptures of various great religions make no such claim at all. There is not the slightest hint in the writings of Confucius that they are a divine revelation. He never dreamed of them as being such. Nor does Buddha claim for his writings any sort of divine revelation. So we see that in many of the great religions of the world no such claim is made; but over two thousand times in the Old Testament alone, the claim is made: "Thus saith the Lord." "Then the word of the Lord came unto Jeremiah the prophet" (Jer. 28:12). Over and over again, "Thus saith the Lord." The claim is made.

Now I will readily grant to anyone that making a claim and substantiating it are two entirely different matters. But if the claim were not even made, then some would no doubt say, "The Christians are claiming for the Bible that which it never claims for itself, namely, to be a revelation from God." You may have heard somebody say sometime, "Well, Jesus never claimed to be the Messiah." Have you ever heard that? Well, that is part of the invincible ignorance that prevails in this country today concerning the Scriptures. Even the most cursory reading of the Gospels would convince someone that that is not the case.

In the fourth chapter of John, the woman at the well says to Christ, "I know that Messiah cometh . . . he will tell us all things." Jesus replied, "I that speak unto thee am he" (John 4:25–26). How much more explicit a claim could you want? He repeated it several more times; and lastly, under oath before the Sanhedrin, when He was asked if He were the Christ, the Son of the living God, He replied, "I am" (Mark 14:62). Well, so also the Scriptures claim to be the Word of God. If the Scriptures didn't make this claim, then some people would say that we were trying to claim for Scripture something that it did not claim for itself.

But then, are we going to demonstrate that this claim is true? The same people who would be likely to make a statement like that are the people who will say, "Well, the Bible is full of contradictions and errors." I'm sure you have heard that many times. I would suggest a simple reply that I have used many times. I simply pull the New Testament out of my coat pocket and say to them, "That is very interesting. I've been studying the Bible for years, and I haven't been able to find one. Would you be so kind as to show me where they are?"

I'm still waiting to be shown. No, the Bible is not full of contradictions and errors; and the people that most facilely make the claim are usually those that know the least about what the Bible teaches. Usually they are people who have never even read it once. We might remind them that, for example, A. T. Robertson, whose massive work *Greek Grammar in Light of Historical Research* is the greatest work on Greek grammar that has ever been written, believed in the absolute infallibility of the Scriptures. Dr. Robert Dick Wilson of Princeton, probably the greatest linguist who ever lived and who knew forty-six different languages, believed that the Old Testament was absolutely trustworthy. W. F. Arndt and F. W. Gingrich, authors of the most modern Greek lexicon that we have today in which every word in the Greek Testament is examined from virtually all of ancient Greek literature, provide the most microscopic examination of the full meaning of all the words in the entire Greek New Testament. Yet these scholars believe absolutely that the Bible is infallibly true and without contradiction in the least. W. F. Arndt's book *Does the Bible Contradict Itself?* takes several of the supposed contradictions mustered by those who have been placed on the spot, and shows that they are only of the most superficial type. Even the most cursory examination beneath the surface shows them to be no contradictions at all. No, the Bible is not full of contradictions and errors, but is, indeed, the Word of God.

How can we prove it? God tells us plainly how we can prove it. How will you know that a prophet is sent from God? God presents us with that same question, and answers it like this: "When a prophet speaketh in the name of the LORD, if the thing follow not nor come to pass, that is the thing which the LORD has not spoken" (Deut. 18:22). The gift of prophecy is one of the methods by which the Bible authenticates itself as the Word of God. Now, some people would again not appreciate the significance of this, because they do not realize that this also is something that is strikingly absent from all other religious writings. For example, the writings of Buddha are totally lacking in any sort of specific predictive prophecy about the things of the future. In the writings of Confucius, there is absolutely no hint of any predictive prophecies. In the case of the Koran, the scriptures of the Muslims, we find only the prophecy of Mohammed that he would return to Mecca, a "self-fulfilling prophecy," which he himself, of course, fulfilled. This is quite different from the prophecy of Christ, who said that He would rise from the dead. And that is just one of several thousands of prophecies that occur in the Scriptures and that are of the most specific, concrete, and definite nature.

The Bible says, "Despise not prophesyings. Prove all things; hold fast that which is good" (1 Thess. 5:20–21). Some people will say, "Oh, well, these prophecies were just vague and general prophecies such as the prophecy of the Delphian Oracle, who prophesied that when two Roman generals met outside the city of Rome to fight a war, the enemy of Rome would be destroyed. Well, both of them took heart in that prophecy, supposing themselves to be the friend of Rome. Obviously that prophecy could not help but be fulfilled one way or the other." Or the skeptics might say, "Well, we have people who prophesy today." Do we? Is that true? Let us take a look. Probably the most notable is Jeane Dixon. Here is a prophet who we are told has made amazing prophecies with astounding accuracy—but we are not told about all of the mistakes! For example, in the decade of the fifties she prophesied all of the candidates of each of the major political parties; and she prophesied the winner of each of three presidential elections, in 1952, 1956, and 1960. How well did she do? Well, by flipping a coin you could have done reasonably well—but her record for that whole decade was zero! She missed every candidate in every party and every winner of every presidential election. That you probably haven't heard before. And so we see that there is a vast jump that separates the prophecies of someone like this from the unfailing prophecies of the Scripture, which have all come to pass as they were supposed to.

Let us take a closer look at them. We see that these prophecies concern many subjects, including two that I would like to look at more thoroughly. We could take the time to examine the life of Christ. There are 333 specific prophecies concerning the life of Christ in the Old Testament, but I assume they are fairly well known.

I would, however, like to look at the fact that almost every major city and virtually every nation within a thousand miles of Israel had its entire future prophesied by the Bible. So these are prophecies so specific, so concrete, so definite, that anybody can tell whether they have been fulfilled. Any high school student with an encyclopedia could check up on them, yet most people simply ignore them or are not even aware of the fact that they exist.

First of all, look at the prophecies concerning the cities of Tyre and Sidon. You might note that the prophecies concerning both cities and nations are of different types. Some prophecies say that the cities and nations will be eradicated. They will be destroyed and they will never again be inhabited. Other cities are to be decimated, put to the sword, but they will continue. Others will be diminished, made base, but they will exist down through the centuries. This is amazing! Suppose these prophecies were reversed. How the skeptics would rejoice with glee! Yet they are unfailingly, infallibly accurate. For example, Tyre was the capital of the world for two thousand years, and it had grown until it had become to the sea what Babylon was to the land. Carthage was but one of the colonies of Tyre when Ezekiel uttered his famous prophecies about this great city. He said this (notice the specific nature of the prophecy): "And they shall destroy the walls of Tyrus, and break down her towers: I will also scrape her dust from her, and make her like the top of a rock. It shall be a place for the spreading of nets in the midst of the sea: for I have spoken it, saith the Lord GOD." "They shall lay thy stones and thy tim-ber and thy dust in the midst of the water." "And I will make thee like the top of a rock . . . thou shalt be built no more: for I the LORD have spoken it" (Ezek. 26:4–5, 12, 14).

Well, what happened? Some years after Ezekiel made his prophecy, Nebuchadnezzar, the mighty monarch of Babylon, invaded the coastal regions and besieged the city of Tyre. For thirteen years, he laid siege to the mighty walls of the city of Tyre until he finally breached them. The horses of Nebuchadnezzar rode into the streets of Tyre, the population was put to the sword, and blood flowed like wine. The city was sacked, a few of the towers were destroyed, a few holes were made in the walls, the city was burned, and Nebuchadnezzar returned to Babylon. Was the prophecy fulfilled (see Ezek. 26:7)? Only in a small part. The city was destroyed, but there, jutting up into the horizon over the bleak Mediterranean, could be seen the remains of the walls and the mighty towers of Tyre. There, within those walls, great piles of huge stones, timbers, and dust bore eloquent testimony to the fact that prophecies were not fulfilled. Yet God had spoken specifically of these things. Who now would ever do what He had prophesied? Who would come and level the walls of this city? Who would come and take the huge stones of this city and dump them into the sea? Who would take the timbers and throw them into the ocean and even scrape the dust until this great mound of rubble would become like a bare rock, a place for the spreading of nets? What madman would do these things? Who would guarantee that this city would be built and inhabited no more?

Note also that Ezekiel did not prophesy after the event; for he died, and another century went by, and another, and another half a century. A quarter of a millennium later, the city still stood there as mute testimony to the fact that the prophecy had not yet been completely fulfilled. And then, like a bugle call, there came a thrill of terror out of the north— as a mighty conqueror appeared on the horizon. Clad in silver, with armor of gold and plumed helmet, astride his mighty

white horse Bucephalus, and followed by the massive pha-
lanxes of Greece came that mighty one whose name was
Alexander the Great—a name which sent shivers of fear
down the spines of those in Persia. There at the Issus he met
the mighty monarch of Persia and dealt him his first crush-
ing blow. The king fled to the south and then to the east.
Before Alexander followed him inland, however, he decided
to nullify the force of the great Persian navy by sealing off all
of its seaports. One by one they surrendered. But then he
came to Tyre, half a mile out in the Mediterranean Sea, built
on an island. How could he get at it? He demanded they surrender. They laughed at him. They were impregnable in their
ocean fortress. Finally, Alexander conceived one of the most
daring and most brilliant schemes in the history of warfare.
He would build a causeway across the half mile of the
Mediterranean Sea, and he would utterly destroy this city
that had thwarted his plans. Where would they find the material? "Tear down the towers! Destroy the walls! Take the
huge stones and the timbers and cast them into the sea!"

Some years ago I picked up a little book called *Alexander
the Great* by Charles Mercer, with consultant Cornelius C.
Vermeule III, the Curator of Classical Art at the Museum of
Fine Arts in Boston. This book includes a most amazing
description: "Mainland Tyre was leveled, and its rubble was
carried to the construction site. Meanwhile, logs were
dragged from the forests of Lebanon, and quarries were
opened in the hills to supply stones for Diades' fabulous high-
way . . . Alexander himself carried stones on his back." Rubble, logs, stones! "They shall lay [Tyre's] stones and thy tim-
ber and thy dust in the midst of the water" (Ezek. 26:12).
Two-and-a-half centuries after that prophecy, it was fulfilled!

Yet still the prophecy was not completely fulfilled, for yet
more was to be done to the city of Tyre. It had been scraped
clean and now was like a rock. It was to become a "place to
spread nets upon" (Ezek. 26:14). Constantin Volney, the great
skeptic, told of seeing fishermen spread their nets there. I,

myself, have seen pictures showing the nets of fishermen spread on the rock of Tyre.

Now compare the prophecies concerning Sidon, a few miles to the north (see Isa. 23; Jer. 27:3–6; 47:4). God said that famine and pestilence would come there and He would send the sword, but the city would continue (see Ezek. 28:23). And so it did! It was never destroyed, although it was sacked and pillaged many times. It continued, despite this plunder, to exist down to our day. Suppose the prophet had gotten his prophecies mixed up!

Take another pair of cities of similar type: Samaria and Jerusalem, the capital of the kingdom of the south and the capital of the kingdom of the north. Concerning Jerusalem, it is well known God stated that He would destroy this city by Nebuchadnezzar—He would tear down its mighty walls (see Jer. 24:9; 29:21; 35:17). But He also said that the walls would be built again, in troublesome times. The walls would be built, and the city would be reinhabited (see Isa. 4:3–6). Of course we all know that is true. I have stood on top of those mighty walls and walked atop part of their length. They are there today, an awesome sight. But what about the great walls of the mighty city of Samaria, built high upon a mountain? Of those walls God said that He would cast down the rocks into the valley below, that He would destroy the city, that He would make it into a vineyard, and that He would uncover the foundations of that city (see Micah 1:5–6). I have visited the city of Samaria, and what did I see? Without even being aware of these particular prophecies, I remember looking over the cliff down thousands of feet below to see the huge boulders that had once been the walls of Samaria. I remember having the various trees and plantings (olive trees and the vineyards) pointed out to us by the guide. Then I saw the great depths of excavations where all of the walls of other centuries, one dynasty after another, had been exposed. The very foundations of Samaria were laid bare! These are but a few of the prophecies concerning cities.

We know that God says concerning cities like Ashdod (which I have also visited) "and I will cut off the inhabitants from Ashdod" (Amos 1:8). Complete and crystal clear definition of the fact that this city is going to be destroyed! There is absolutely nothing living there—it is complete and total desolation. There is not the first house or shack or tent where once Ashdod was (see Zeph. 2:4).

The same is true of Ashkelon. "Ashkelon shall be a desolation. It shall not be inhabited" (Zech. 9:5). Today, almost twenty-five hundred years later, Ashkelon is still uninhabited and still a desolation! This is attested by Constantin Volney, who refers to "the deserted ruins of Azkalan" (*Volney's Travels*, 2:338).

If you feel that those interpretations are subjective, let me point out to you that I am using as reference the writings of various skeptics garnered from the collection of Dr. Alexander Keith. Skeptics quoted are such men as Constantin Volney, who made Abraham Lincoln into a skeptic for most of his earlier years, and Edward Gibbon, the author of *The Rise and Fall of the Roman Empire*, who was a notorious skeptic.

All of the cities of Edom were to be destroyed. The prophecies are striking and specific. Jeremiah says, "And Edom [or Idumea] shall be a desolation . . . As in the overthrow of Sodom and Gomorrah and the neighbor cities thereof, saith the LORD, no man shall abide there, neither shall a son of man dwell in it" (Jer. 49:17–18). Ezekiel is even more emphatic. He declares that because Edom, or Mount Seir (the Mount of Edom), had fought against the Israelites in the time of their calamity, God will utterly destroy them. He says, "Thus saith the Lord GOD; Behold, O Mount Seir, I am against thee, and I will stretch out mine hand against thee, and I will make thee most desolate. I will lay thy cities waste, and thou shalt be desolate, and thou shalt know that I am the LORD." "I will make thee perpetual desolations, and thy cities shall not return: and ye shall know that I am the LORD" (Ezek. 35:3–4, 9). Ezekiel further describes the extent of the desolation which shall fall upon the land of Edom, "I will also stretch out mine hand upon Edom, and . . . I will make it desolate from Teman" (Ezek. 25:13).

These are startling prophecies. They are exceedingly specific. No one is to live in these cities, no son is to be born in them, and the cities shall not return. Thus we will know that the Lord is God. The extent of the desolation both geographically and chronologically is described. Here is a bold gauntlet thrown down before unbelievers. Have these spectacular prophecies come to pass? Listen to the writings of various skeptics and other travelers in the Near East. Concerning Edom, Constantin Volney says that the traces of many towns and villages are met with. At present all this country is a desert. Also concerning Edom, John L. Burckhardt declares, "And Maan is the only inhabited place in it" (*Burckhardt's Travels*, 436). Even the nature of the desolation is described by Jeremiah. "If grapegatherers come to thee, would they not leave some gleaning grapes? If thieves by night, they will destroy till they have enough. But I have made Esau [Edom] bare" (Jer. 49:9–10). Burckhardt declares that the whole plain presented to the view "an expanse of shifting sands, the depth of sand precludes all vegetation of herbage" (*Burckhardt's Travels*, 442). According to the prophet, cities of Mount Edom, or Mount Seir, were to be ruined and laid waste. According to Burckhardt, "The following ruined places are situated in Mount Seir, Kalaab, Djirba, Eyl, Ferdakh, Anyk, Birel-Beytar, Shemakh, and Syk" (*Burchkardt's Travels*, 443–44). Commenting on the statement that by this desolation, "ye shall know that I am the LORD" (Ezek. 6:7), Stephen, a Christian standing among the ruins of Petra, the capital of Edom, declares, "I would that the skeptic could stand as I did among the ruins of this city, among the rocks, and there open the Sacred Book, and read the words of the inspired penmen, written when this desolate place was one of the greatest cities in the world. I see the scoff arrested, his cheek pale, his lip quivering, and his heart quaking with fear, as the ruined city cries out to him in a voice loud and powerful as that of one risen from the dead. Though he would not believe Moses and the prophets, he believes the handwriting of God Himself and the desolation and eternal ruin around him" (*Stephen's Incidents of Travel in Arabia*. Petraea).

Let us now look at some of the even larger examples of the prophecies of God concerning whole nations and their capital cities. Examine the city of Nineveh, the capital of the great Assyrian Empire. Nineveh conquered the world of its day. Concerning this city and nation, God makes some very specific declarations. He says, "But with an overrunning flood he will make an utter end of the place thereof." And "I will make thy grave; for thou art vile" (Nah. 1:8, 14). The prophet said, as he looked into the future, "She is empty, and void, and waste." And "no more of thy name be sown" (Nah. 2:10; 1:14). Interesting prophecies. What happened? Nineveh was taken away, just as God had said.

How was this done? Exactly in the manner that God had prophesied. Nahum the prophet declared, "They shall make haste to the wall thereof, and the defense shall be prepared. The gates of the rivers shall be opened, and the palace shall be dissolved" (Nah. 2:5–6). Further, "The gates of thy land shall be set wide open unto thy enemies: the fire shall devour thy bars" (Nah. 3:13). Notice the details of these prophecies. The Ninevites are to flee in haste to the great defensive walls of their city, which are prepared for any attack. But the gates of the rivers will be opened and will dissolve the palace. This results in the gates of the land being set wide open to the enemies and fire devouring the city. The only detailed historical account of the fall of Nineveh is the account of Ctesias, preserved in *Diodorus Siculus*. According to that account, Cyaxares (the Median monarch), aided by the Babylonians under Nabopolassar, laid siege to the city. His efforts were in vain. He was more than once repulsed and was obliged to take refuge in the mountains of the Zagros Range; but, receiving reinforcements, he succeeded in routing the Assyrian army and driving them to shut themselves up within the walls. He then attempted to reduce the city by blockade, but was unsuccessful for two years until his efforts were unexpectedly assisted by an extraordinary rise of the Tigris, which swept away a part of the walls and rendered it possible for the Medes to enter. The Assyrian monarch Saracus burned himself in his palace in despair. With the ruthless barbarity of the times, the conquerors gave the whole city over to the flames and razed its former magnificence to the ground (*Cyclopedia of Biblical, Theological, and Ecclesiastical Literature,* 7:112). God makes clear that the destruction of this city will be total and irremediable. He says, "But with an overrunning flood he will make an utter end to the place thereof, and darkness shall pursue his enemies" (Nah. 1:8). The city was then laid waste, its monuments destroyed, and its inhabitants scattered or carried away into captivity. It never rose again from its ruins. This total disappearance of Nineveh is fully confirmed by the records of history.

The prophet Nahum also said of Nineveh, "She is empty, and void, and waste" (Nah. 2:10). The skeptic Edward Gibbon described the complete fulfillment of this prophecy when he detailed a battle fought on the very site where Nineveh had once stood. He said that eastward of the Tigris, at the end of the bridge of Mosul, the great Nineveh had formerly been erected. The city and even the ruins had long since disappeared; the vacant space afforded a spacious field for the operation of the two armies (*Gibbon's History,* 8:250–51). God had also said, "I will make thy grave; for thou art vile" (Nah. 1:14). The mounds show neither bricks, stones, nor other materials of building, but are in many places overgrown with grass (*Buckingham's Travels in Mesopotamia,* 2:49). God had said that He would literally wipe Nineveh off the face of the earth and make an utter end of it (Nah. 1:9). In unknowing confirmation of the fulfillment of that prophecy, Constantin Volney cries, "Where are those ramparts of Nineveh? The name of Nineveh seems to be threatened with the same oblivion that has overtaken its greatness" (*Volney's Ruins,* chaps. 2, 4). E. A. Rowell has said that never had the world seen such a city. Its great rampart walls towered upward two hundred feet, and on top several chariots could race abreast. Gleaming in the sun, its lofty palaces and temple towers stabbed the sky above the towering walls and thrilled the approaching traveler while he was yet miles away.

The city was so completely destroyed that the Romans in A.D. 627 under Heraclius fought a battle on top of Nineveh and didn't even know it was there, and for well over a thousand years few people even believed that it had ever existed. As recently as 1840, the writings of skeptics are filled with delusions that Nineveh and Sargon and Ashurbanipal, the great kings of Assyria, are all mythological characters—some of the many "mistakes" of the Bible—because, as every educated person knows, Nineveh never existed, Assyria never was. "Their place is not known." "That no more of thy name be sown" (Nah. 3:17; 1:14). It wasn't until 1840 that someone discovered a brick in the midst of the mounds near the Tigris River that had on it the name of Sargon, king of Assyria. It was taken to the Paris Museum where they said it was obviously a fraud because everybody knows there was no Nineveh, so there was no Sargon! But in 1845 Layard, who was to become the greatest Assyriologist of all time, had the audacity to uncover the palace, the library, and the whole city. The critics were forced to admit that Nineveh had existed after all.

Consider the magnificent kingdom that followed it: Babylonia. Babylon was probably the greatest city that was ever built. Here was the magnificent temple of Belus, and here were the world famous Hanging Gardens.

Babylon drew her stores from no foreign country. She invented an alphabet; worked out problems of arithmetic; invented implements for measuring time; conceived the plan of building enormous structures with the poorest of all materials—clay; discovered the art of polishing, boring, and engraving gems; studied successfully the motions of the heavenly bodies; conceived of grammar as a science; elaborated a system of law; saw the value of exact chronology. In almost every branch of science, she made a beginning. Much of the art and learning of Greece came from Babylon. But of this majestic kingdom, this Babylon the Golden, God said, "Babylon, the glory of kingdoms, the beauty of the Chaldees' excellency, shall be as when God overthrew Sodom and Gomorrah" (Isa. 13:19). This is but one of over one hundred specific prophecies that are made concerning Babylon alone. The specificity of these prophecies is so great that they cannot possibly be said to be obscure as in the Delphic Oracles. Nor can they be said to have been written after the event, because many of the details of the prophecies were not fulfilled until centuries after the Septuagint translation of the Hebrew Old Testament into Greek in 150 B.C. It is not possible to give a later date for these prophecies. Nor can it be said that they have not been fulfilled, for any schoolboy with a good encyclopedia can ascertain that they have been minutely fulfilled. In these prophecies concerning the future of great cities and kingdoms, God has written His imprimatur in the Scriptures, confirming them as divine revelations in such bold letters that He that runneth may read (Ps. 147:15). Nor can it be said that they are simply lucky guesses, because there are thousands of such prophecies in the Scriptures that have been minutely fulfilled. Nor yet can it be said that they concern events that were likely to take place. Indeed, many of the events were totally without precedent in the history of the world and were so incredible and unbelievable in their very nature that even though history has fully confirmed them to be true, we still stagger at the audacity of the prophets who made such bold statements.

Consider the great walls of Babylon. Herodotus tells us that these walls had towers which extended above the 200-foot walls to a height of 300 feet. The walls were 187 feet thick at the base and were 14 miles square, according to one ancient authority. The triple walls of Babylon were the mightiest walls that were ever built around any city. Concerning these walls God says, in Jeremiah 51:58, "The broad walls of Babylon shall be utterly broken." Also, "And they shall not take of thee a stone for a corner, nor a stone for foundations; but thou shalt be desolate for ever" (Jer. 51:26). Consider these astounding facts: (1) The wall is to be broken down; (2) it is to be broken down completely; (3) it is to be broken down permanently. It cannot possibly be said that these prophecies did not come to pass. Even the skeptics attest their fulfillment. "Where are the walls of Babylon?" asks Constantin Volney in his *Ruins*. Major Keppel said in his *Narrative* that in common with other travelers, we totally failed in discovering any trace of the city walls.

Nor can anyone say that the prophecy was made after the event, for the walls were not suddenly destroyed. The city was taken by stealth by the Medes and Persians, and the destruction of her walls was a slow process that took centuries. The walls were still in existence in the time of Alexander the Great. They still jutted into the sky at the time of Christ. In the fourth century A.D., some remains of the walls were still there, a stark reminder that the prophecy had not yet been completely fulfilled. Then the most astounding event took place. Julian the Apostate, Emperor of Rome, determined to rid the Roman Empire of Christianity and to reestablish paganism, was doing all in his power to destroy belief in the Scriptures. However, God had said that even "the wrath of man shall praise [Him]" (Ps. 76:10). While engaged in a war with the Persians near the remains of Babylon (although he had no idea of the prophecy that he was fulfilling), Julian completely destroyed the remnants of the wall of Babylon lest it afford any protection in the future for the Persian army. And thus the prophecy was brought to fulfillment by one of the greatest antagonists of Scripture of all time.

One cannot say it was inevitable that the wall would be destroyed. The Great Wall of China is not nearly as large or as strong, and yet, though it is older, it still stands today. The walls of Jerusalem and many other ancient cities, though destroyed many times in part, have been rebuilt and still remain to our time. I have personally walked atop the great walls of Jerusalem, which God said would be destroyed, but also He said that they would be built again in troublous times. In the case of the Babylonian wall and the Jerusalem wall, exactly what God said has come to pass (see Jer. 39:8; Dan. 9:25; Micah 7:11; Isa. 33:20).

When Babylon was the mistress of the world, containing within its mighty walls 196 square miles of the most magnificently developed city of all time, with beautiful parks, lakes, aqueducts, and hanging gardens, the prophet Jeremiah made this astounding prophecy: "Because of the wrath of the LORD it shall not be inhabited, but it shall be wholly desolate" (Jer. 50:13). Even more astonishing is the further prophecy of Jeremiah: "And it shall be no more inhabited for ever; neither shall it be dwelt in from generation to generation" (Jer. 50:39). This was an astonishing prophecy, for it was virtually without precedent. Many ancient cities in the Near East had been destroyed, but always they had been built again on the ruins of the previous cities. There is evidence of sometimes twenty or thirty cities being built on the very same site. Babylon was most excellently situated on the Euphrates. It had fine possibilities of commerce. It was militarily almost invincible. Its fields were so fertile that Herodotus, having visited there, was afraid to describe what he saw lest he be thought insane.

Have these astonishing prophecies been fulfilled? Babylon was described as the tenantless sand desolate metropolis (*Mignan's Travels*, 234), a barren desert in which the ruins were nearly the only indication that it had been inhabited. Regarding Babylon, Isaiah said, "Neither shall it be dwelt in from generation to generation" (Isa. 13:20). In the sixteenth century, there was not a house to be seen at Babylon (*Ray's Collection of Travels*, Rawolf, 174). In the nineteenth century, it was still desolate and tenantless (*Mignan's Travels*, 284). In the twentieth century, ruins are all that remain of the once magnificent city where King Belshazzar saw the handwriting on the wall (John Elder, *Prophets and Diggers*, 106). "It shall never be inhabited," prophesied Isaiah (Isa. 13:20). Ruins like those of Babylon composed of heaps of rubbish impregnated with niter cannot be cultivated (*Rich's Memoirs*, 16). The decomposing materials of a Babylonian structure doom the earth on which they perish to a lasting sterility (*Sir R. K. Porter's Travels*, 2:391). Thus God guaranteed the fulfillment of His prophecies: "Thou [Babylon] shalt be desolate for ever." And "Babylon shall become heaps, a dwelling place for dragons, an astonishment, and an hissing, without an inhabitant" (Jer. 51:26, 37).

There are other amazingly specific details in this prophecy. Consider this detail: "Neither shall the Arabian pitch tent there." Has this come true? Captain Mignan said that he saw the sun sink behind the Mujelibah, and obeyed with infinite regret the summons of his guides, who were completely armed. He could not persuade them to remain longer. From the apprehension of evil spirits, it is impossible to eradicate this idea from the minds of these people (*Mignan's Travels*, 2, 198, 201). Continues Isaiah: "Neither shall the shepherds make their fold there" (Isa. 13:20). All the people of the country assert that it is extremely dangerous to approach this mound after nightfall on account of the multitude of evil spirits by which it is haunted. By this superstitious belief they are prevented from pitching a tent by night or making a fold (*Rich's Memoirs*, 27).

Consider these two specific, but apparently contradictory, prophecies. "The sea is come up upon Babylon: she is covered with the multitude of the waves thereof." And, "Her cities are a desolation, a dry land and a wilderness" (Jer. 51:42–43). Now note the amazing fulfillment. For the space of two months throughout the year, the ruins of Babylon are inundated by the annual overflowing of the Euphrates so as to render many parts of them inaccessible by converting the valleys into morasses (*Rich's Memoirs*, 13). After the subsiding of the waters, even the low heaps become again sunburnt ruins; and the sight of Babylon, like that of the other cities of Chaldea, is a dry waste, a parched and burning plain (*Buckingham's Travels*, 2:302–5).

In spite of the unimaginable fertility of the plains around Babylon, God had said, "Cut off the sower from Babylon, and him that handleth the sickle in the time of harvest" (Jer. 50:16). On this part of the plain, both where traces of buildings were left and where none had stood, all seemed equally naked of vegetation (*Porter's Travels*, 2:392). "And Babylon shall become heaps" (Jer. 51:37). And again, "Cast her up as heaps, and destroy her utterly: let nothing of her be left" (Jer. 50:26). Babylon has become a vast succession of mounds, a great mass of ruined heaps (*Keppel's Narrative*, 1:196).

These prophecies are presented here as examples of the over one hundred specific prophecies relating to the city of Babylon. The wrath of the Lord was poured out upon Babylon. God said, "The LORD . . . will do his pleasure on Babylon" (Isa. 48:14). God said, "The Lord . . . for every purpose of the LORD shall be performed against Babylon. And I will bring upon that land all my words which I have pronounced against it, even all that is written in this book" (Jer. 51:29). Let us close this discussion of Babylon with the words of one who looked with his own eyes upon the fulfillment of these prophecies. "I cannot portray," says Captain Mignan, "the overpowering sensation of reverential awe that possessed my mind while contemplating the extent and magnitude of ruin and devastation on every side" (*Mignan's Travels*, 117).

Thus God threw down the gauntlet to all unbelievers. Do you want to disprove the Scriptures? It is very easy! Simply rebuild Babylon! God said it would never be inhabited, it would never be rebuilt, but it would always remain a desolation. There was a man who set out to rebuild it. I should tell you about him. He had all the wealth of the whole world at his command. His name was Alexander the Great. After conquering the world, he decided to have a trade route by sea from Babylon to Egypt, and he decided to make Babylon his central headquarters for his worldwide empire. He issued six hundred thousand rations to his soldiers to rebuild the city of Babylon. Alexander the Great, the ruler of the world, said, "Rebuild Babylon!" and God struck him dead! He was immediately taken with a fever, and within a few days he was dead. The ruins of Babylon still stand in mute testimony. I, the Lord, have spoken it! "It shall never be inhabited again!" (Jer. 50:39).

Compare these prophecies of destruction with what the Bible says about Egypt. God said that Nineveh, Assyria, and Babylonia would be completely destroyed and not be rebuilt. What if He had said that about Egypt? Ah, how the skeptics would laugh. But He didn't. "They shall be there a base kingdom. It shall be the basest of the kingdoms; neither shall it exalt itself any more above the nations: for I will diminish them, that they shall no more rule over the nations" (Ezek. 29:14–15). "The pride of her power shall come down. . . . And they shall be desolate in the midst of the countries that are desolate, and her cities shall be in the midst of the cities that are wasted" (Ezek. 30:6–7). "And I will make the land of Egypt desolate" (Ezek. 29:12), "and the country shall be destitute of that whereof it was full" (Ezek. 32:15), "and there shall be no more a prince of the land of Egypt" (30:13).

Let us note that the fate of Egypt is not, as in the case of Nineveh and Babylon, to be utter extinction, but rather "they shall be there." Egypt was to continue to exist as a nation but as "a base kingdom," "the basest of kingdoms" (Ezek. 29:14–15). It is to be diminished and emptied of that whereof it was full. Have these prophecies been fulfilled? After the defeat of Antony, Augustus found such great wealth in Egypt that out of it he paid all of the arrears of his army and all of the debts that he had incurred during the war. Still he feared that the wealth of Egypt would present to him a rival. For six hundred more years Alexandria continued to be the first city in the Roman Empire in rank, commerce, and prosperity. A hundred years later the Muslim hordes attacked Egypt and conquered it. They were overwhelmed by the sight of the city's magnificence and wealth. Future invaders were equally astonished at the wealth of Egypt, until the nation was reduced to a state of abject poverty, finally being brought to the place of international bankruptcy that brought about the Anglo-French dominion of Egypt.

One of the most astonishing parts of the prophecy is the statement, "There shall be no more a prince of the land of Egypt" (Ezek. 30:13). This prophecy is particularly striking when we note that for approximately two thousand years before the prophecy was made, Egypt had had Egyptian princes sitting upon its throne. It seemed as if it would continue forever. But God declares that there shall no more be a prince of the land of Egypt. What a startling declaration! There has been ample time for the testing of the prophecy, for there continued to be a prince on the throne of Egypt until the last several decades, when a democratic form of government was accepted. But were any of these princes Egyptians? Let us have that question answered by the pens of skeptics and infidels. Constantin Volney said that, deprived 2300 years ago of her natural proprietors, Egypt has seen her fertile fields successively a prey to the Persians, the Macedonians, the Romans, the Greeks, the Arabs, the Georgians, and at length the race of Tartars, distinguished by the name of Ottoman Turks. The Mamelukes soon usurped the power and elected a leader (*Volney's Travels*, 1:74, 103, 110, 193). After Volney's time, Mohammed Ali established the princedom again in Egypt, but he was not himself an Egyptian. Rather he was born at Kavala, a small seaport on the frontier of Thrace and Macedonia. His father was an Albanian aga. After this, Egypt was ruled by the French and the English. The skeptic Edward Gibbon confirms this testimony, stating that a more unjust and absurd constitution cannot be devised than that which condemns the natives of a country to perpetual servitude under the arbitrary dominion of strangers and slaves (Gibbon, *The Decline and Fall of the Roman Empire*, chap. 59).

Today Egypt, which has for two millennia suffered under the despotic hand of strangers, has been reduced to one of the basest of nations. My guide to the Holy Land a few years ago said that he had been to Egypt thirty or forty times, but he was never going back again because it was so foul, so vile smelling, so poverty ridden, that he couldn't stand another trip. His stomach couldn't take the cities of Egypt anymore. I will make thee "the basest of kingdoms" (Ezek. 29:15).

These are but a few of the thousands of prophecies with which the Scripture abounds, which are found in no other religious writings of the world, and which are clear evidence that the Scripture has been written by the hand of God.

> How firm a foundation, ye saints of the Lord,
> Is laid for your faith in his excellent Word!
> What more can he say than to you He hath said?

"I am God, and there is none like me, declaring the end from the beginning, and from ancient times the things that are not yet done" (Isa. 46:9–10). The Bible, and no other book, unfailingly and infallibly tells of the future. The Scriptures are the Word of God. "Sanctify them through thy truth," said Christ, "thy word is truth" (John 17:17).

The Scriptures cannot be broken!

Scripture Index